THE FOUR BIGGEST MISTAKES IN OPTION TRADING

SECOND EDITION

JAY KAEPPEL

ISBN 1-59280-255-9
ISBN 978-1-59280-255-5
Printed in the United States of America.

Contents

INTRODUCTION   vii

Mistake #1
RELYING SOLELY ON MARKET TIMING TO TRADE OPTIONS   1
Why Traders Make Mistake #1   1
Why Mistake #1 Causes Losses In The Long Run   12
How To Avoid Mistake #1   22

Mistake #2
BUYING ONLY OUT-OF-THE-MONEY OPTIONS   27
Why Traders Make Mistake #2   29
Why Mistake #2 Causes Losses In The Long Run   34
How To Avoid Mistake #2   42

Mistake #3
USING STRATEGIES THAT ARE TOO COMPLEX   47
Why Traders Make Mistake #3   48
Why Mistake #3 Causes Losses In The Long Run   55
How To Avoid Mistake #3   64

Mistake #4
CASTING TOO WIDE OF A NET   67
Why Traders Make Mistake #4   67
Why Mistake #4 Causes Losses In The Long Run   67
How To Avoid Mistake #4   77

SUMMARY   81

ABOUT THE AUTHOR AND OPTIONETICS   83
Company Information   85

TRADING SOURCE GUIDE
Tools For Success In Options Trading   87

INTRODUCTION

Options offer traders and investors a number of unique and outstanding opportunities that are not available to those who trade only the underlying stock or futures contracts. A bullish speculator can choose to buy a call option for a fraction of the cost of purchasing the underlying security. Likewise, a bearish speculator can buy a put option. In either case, the speculator enjoys the potential for unlimited profits with limited risk. Other traders may employ strategies that offer an extremely high probability of profit. Many opportunities exist for well-educated traders to craft option positions that make a profit if the underlying security stays within a particular price range, or if it remains above or below a given price. This ability to make money in neutral market situations is something that is available only to option traders. In addition, investors can use options to hedge existing stock or futures positions. Through the astute use of options, investors can mitigate or, in certain cases, virtually eliminate the risk of loss for a position that they hold in a given stock or futures contract. Investors can also use option-hedging strategies to generate additional income from an existing portfolio of stocks.

Yet, despite all of these potential benefits, it is commonly estimated that 90% of option traders lose money in the long run. This staggering figure raises several extremely relevant questions:

1. What is it about option trading that causes so many people to fail?

2. Is there a way to avoid the apparently huge pitfalls that claim so many traders?

3. If the failure rate is so high, why does anybody bother trading options in the first place?

After listening to a multitude of traders talk about their ideas on trading options over the years, it is interesting to note that there are several common themes running through many of these discussions. This raises an interesting question. If 90% of option traders lose money, and a lot of traders subscribe to the same ideas, can one gain an edge by avoiding the common approaches used by these traders?

In order to attempt to answer this question, I systematically tested the option trading approaches most commonly mentioned by traders—especially novice traders—using computer simulations.

As I will detail in the following sections, there are several common pitfalls that the majority of option traders fall into that cause them to lose money in the long run. As we often find to be the case in the realm of investing, whenever "the crowd" migrates to an idea or set of ideas, it usually pays off handsomely (in the long run) to go the other way and simply avoid whatever the crowd is doing. The good news is that by isolating the mistakes most commonly made by option traders, learning why they are so common, why they cause losses in the long run, and how they can be avoided in the future, you take a major step toward becoming a consistently profitable option trader.

There are good trading ideas and bad trading ideas. One of the best ways to find the good ideas is to first eliminate the bad ones. This is what I will attempt to accomplish in the following discussions where we will focus on the four biggest (and most common) mistakes made by the majority of option traders. So consider this the "how not to" portion of your option trading education.

For each of the following four biggest mistakes in option trading, I will first discuss what the mistake is. It is important to have a clear understanding of each error in order to be able to recognize in the future when you might be about to fall into a potential problem situation. I will then explain why it is so common for traders to make this mistake and why it causes traders to lose money in the long run. The idea here is to help you understand the reasons behind why a seemingly enticing idea can lead to your downfall in the long run. But, if you can learn how to avoid making these mistakes, you will stop falling victim to the siren song of tried and failed ideas. Finally, I will detail what needs to be done in order to avoid each of the most common mistakes. The goal here is to teach you to think independently of the "the crowd" and to teach you how to achieve the success that most option traders can only dream about.

One word of warning: a lot of traders may not enjoy reading these sections for the simple reason that we are about to de-bunk several ideas that many hold near and dear. Much of what you are about to read details the way that the majority of option traders trade. Yet, given the fact that most uneducated option traders lose money, it is important to read these sections with an open mind. Most often when someone attacks an idea that you believe to be true, or which "conventional wisdom" has convinced you is true, the first reaction is to become defensive and to try to defend your reasons for believing the idea in the first place. It is impossible to overemphasize the importance of reading the following text with an open mind if you want to trade options profitably in the long run. This is especially true given the following paradox: in most cases, the very ideas that lure traders into the options market in the first place are the same ideas that cause them, in the long run, to lose their time and money.

THE FOUR BIGGEST MISTAKES IN OPTION TRADING

Mistake #1
Relying Solely on Market Timing To Trade Options

WHY TRADERS MAKE MISTAKE #1

Far too many first-time option traders view options as nothing more than a tool for leveraging their market timing decisions. That is, rather than buying or selling short a particular stock or futures contract, they feel that they can buy a call or put option and:

- Commit a great deal less capital than they would to buy the underlying security itself, and,

- Obtain a great deal more leverage than they would if they simply bought the underlying security.

And, in fact, it is possible to attain these benefits via option trading. By putting a relatively small sum of money into an option position, it is possible for a trader to achieve a much higher rate of return on a given trade than if he or she had bought or sold short the underlying security directly. For example, consider a stock that is trading at a price of $55 per share. In order to buy 100 shares of that stock, the investor would need to invest $5,500 (100 shares times $55 per share).

At the same time, a call option with a strike price of 55—which gives the buyer of the option the right, but not the obligation, to buy 100 shares of the underlying stock at a price of $55 a share—might be trading at a price of $3 per contract. In order to buy one call option, the investor need only to put up $300 ($3 per contract times 100). The call option trader's breakeven price in this example is $58 per share (the strike price of 55 plus the premium paid of $3). Hence, the call makes a profit at any stock price above 58. So in this case, the option trader needs to put up only about 5.4% as much capital as the buyer of 100 shares of stock; at any price above $58 per share, the option trader will enjoy point-for-point profit with the more traditional stock trader who invested $5,500 to buy the stock.

That is the good news. Unfortunately, a vast number of market timers adopt the belief that market timing is all they need in order to profit from trading options. Accordingly, they do little or no options analysis—instead adopting the attitude that "if my timing is good, any old option will do." This is invariably a fatal error in the long run.

Market timers take great comfort in their winning trades— perhaps too much comfort. Any winning trades that they experience serve to reinforce their belief that market timing is all that is required in order to succeed, regardless of how few and far between the winning trades may be. Unfortunately, occasionally achieving a high rate of return on a given trade is not the same thing as making money in the long run. The question to ask is not, "Do I achieve a big winner now and then?" (as even the worst traders can occasionally hit a big winner). The relevant question is, "Am I following an approach that is likely to generate profits over the long run?" Traders who rely solely on market timing to trade options must answer no to this all-important question.

The primary reason that relying solely on market timing to trade options fails in the long run is that it completely ignores one of the most important factors in option trading: implied volatility. Before proceeding to explain why market timing alone fails option traders in the long run, let's first discuss what implied volatility is and why an understanding of this important concept is critical to option trading success.

Implied Volatility Defined

The "implied volatility" value for a given option is the value that a trader would need to plug into an option pricing model in order to make the theoretical option price generated by the model equal to the current market price of a particular option. This can be accomplished when the other variables—underlying price, days until option expiration, interest rates, and the difference between the option's strike price and the price of the underlying security—are known. In other words, it is the volatility "implied" by the current market price for a given option. Before proceeding it is important to understand just what implied volatility represents, why it is so important, and the impact that changes in implied volatility can have on your trades.

Calculating Implied Volatility for a Given Option

There are several variables that are entered into an option-pricing model to arrive at a theoretical price, or the "fair value," of a given option:

A) The current price of the underlying security.

B) The strike price of the option under analysis.

C) Current interest rates.

D) The number of days until the option expires.

E) A volatility value.

For stock options, dividends also factor into the model. However, to simplify things here, we will leave dividends out of the following example.

- Elements A through E above are passed to an option-pricing model, which then generates, a theoretical option price.

- Elements A, B, C and D are "known" variables. In other words, at any given point in time one can readily observe the price of the underlying stock (or futures contract), the strike price for the option in question, the current level of interest rates, and the number of days left until the option expires.

Example of Implied Volatility Calculation

To calculate the implied volatility of a given option, we follow this procedure with one important modification. Instead of passing elements A through E to an option pricing model that generates a "theoretical" price, we pass elements A through D along with the actual market price for the option as variable F, and allow the option pricing model to solve for element E, the volatility value. A computer is needed to make this calculation. This volatility value is called the "implied volatility" for that option. In other words, it is the volatility that is implied by the marketplace based on the actual price of the option.

For example, on April 6th the IBM July 2006 85-call option was trading at a price of $2.40. The known variables are:

A) The current price of the underlying
   security = 83.70

B) The strike price of the option under analysis = 85

C) Current interest rate = 3.5

D) The number of days until the option expires = 106

E) Implied volatility = ?

F) The actual market price of the option = 2.40

The unknown variable that must be solved for is element E, volatility. Given the variables listed above, a volatility of 14.21 must be plugged into element E in order for the option-pricing model to generate a theoretical price that equals the actual market price of $2.40. Thus, the "implied volatility" for the IBM July 2006 85-call as of April 6th option is 14.21.

Different options may trade at different implied volatility levels. If demand in the marketplace is great for a given option, the price of that option may be driven to artificially high levels, thus generating a higher implied volatility for that option. The differences in implied volatilities across strike prices among options of the same expiration month for a given underlying are referred to as the volatility "skew." There are a number of different options strategies that are geared to exploit specific volatility skews.

Why Implied Volatility Matters

The actual price of an option, the premium, is the sum of two quantities: intrinsic and extrinsic value. Intrinsic value represents the amount by which the option's strike price is in-the-money (ITM). Extrinsic value represents time premium. If an option is out-of-the-money, then the price is comprised solely of time premium, or extrinsic value. The amount of time premium built into any option is directly related to the amount of time left until expiration and the implied volatility for that option. As a result, the higher the current level of implied volatility, the higher the price for the option. Conversely, the lower the current level of implied volatility, the lower the price for the option. This has obvious ramifications for any trader considering buying or writing a particular option. If you buy a given call option when implied volatility is high, you will pay more for the option than you would if implied volatility was low. This in turn implies that you:

- Will spend more to buy the call option;
- Will have a greater dollar risk;
- Will have a higher breakeven price basis the underlying stock for a call option and a lower breakeven price for a put; and,
- May experience a meaningful decline in the price of the option if there is subsequently a significant decline in volatility.

Let's illustrate these factors further with an example. As you can see in Figure 1, over the course of the past five years, the implied volatility for IBM options with more than 90 days left until expiration has ranged from a low of 13 to a high of 54.

To understand the significance of changes in implied volatility, take a look at how the price of the July 85-call option changes given different implied volatility levels as of April 6th (see Table 1). First, let's look at the low end. If the IBM July 85-call option

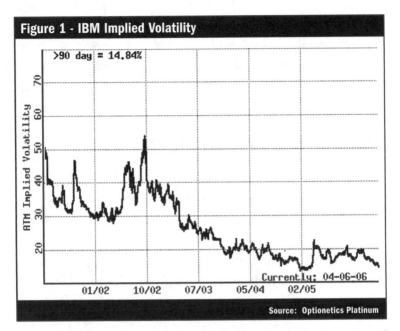

Figure 1 - IBM Implied Volatility

were to trade at an implied volatility level of 13, the price of the option would be $2.30. If the option traded at the two-year high for implied volatility of 24, the price of the option would be $4.28. Finally, if the implied volatility for the option were at the five-year high of 54, the price of the option would be $9.65. These differences have significant implications.

It should be clear from the information contained in Table 1 that implied volatility is a critical piece of information for any option trader to consider. Likewise, any trader who completely ignores implied volatility—for example, one who focuses only

Table 1 - Changes in Implied Volatility = Price Shifts			
July 85-Call Volatility and Price	Underlying Breakeven Price	% Move Required to Reach Breakeven Price	% Probability of Reaching Breakeven Price
13% / 2.30	87.30	4.3%	31%
24% / 4.28	89.28	6.7%	21%
54 / 9.65	94.65	13.1%	6%

on market timing to trade options—will undoubtedly at times be flying blind. This will lead him to buy options in situations where it is not prudent to do so due to high volatility or writing options when it is not a prudent course of action due to low volatility.

Why Implied Volatility Fluctuates

Much of the fluctuation that occurs for an option price is directly related to changes in the price of the underlying security. Clearly, if a stock makes a huge move up, call prices will increase and put prices will decline across the board for that stock. However, the amount of time premium built into a given option is also determined to a great extent by the current level of implied volatility. As we saw in Figure 1, implied volatility levels can change dramatically. Why is this? There are two primary factors – the volatility of the underlying stock and investor perceptions of future volatility.

In order for any option trade to occur, there must be one buyer and one seller, or "writer." Consider this: if out-of-the-money options had no time premium—in other words, if they were all priced at $0.00—why would anyone assume the risk of writing an out-of-the-money option? The amount of time premium built into each option is essentially the inducement available to a trader to take the risk of writing that option. When the underlying stock price starts to behave in a volatile manner, or if some impending news situation causes investors to think that volatility will rise in the near future, then option writers will essentially demand higher premiums before they will be willing to take the risk of writing options on that stock. This demand for higher premiums is reflected by a higher implied volatility value.

Implied Volatility for a Given Security

While each option for a given market may trade at its own implied volatility level, it is possible to objectively arrive at a single value to refer to as the average implied volatility value for the options of a given security for a specific day. This daily value can then be compared to the historical range of implied volatility values for that security to determine if this current reading is "high" or "low."

Figure 2 displays the implied volatility values for IBM options for different timeframes. Typically shorter-term options are more volatile than longer-term options. This is clearly reflected in the various lines that appear in Figure 2, which displays 24 months of implied volatility history.

One way to reduce the amount of "noise" is to only consider options with 90 days or more left until expiration. Figure 3

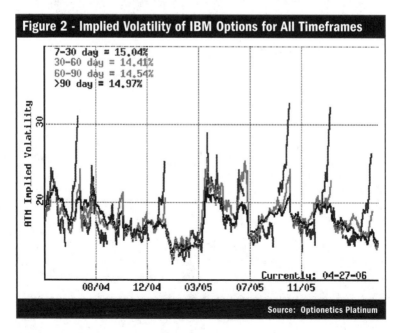

Figure 2 - Implied Volatility of IBM Options for All Timeframes

7-30 day = 15.04%
30-60 day = 14.41%
60-90 day = 14.54%
>90 day = 14.97%

ATM Implied Volatility

Currently: 04-27-06

08/04   12/04   03/05   07/05   11/05

Source: Optionetics Platinum

displays the implied volatility for IBM options with 90 or more days left until expiration for the prior 24 months.

As you can see in Figures 1, 2 and 3, the implied volatility for the options of a given security can fluctuate widely over a period of time. Also, each stock and futures market establishes its own range of highs and lows for implied volatility. Without knowing the range of volatility levels for each security, it is impossible to compare apples to apples when comparing two or more underlying securities. In Figure 4, note how the implied volatility for options on Amazon.com stock has ranged from 28% to 172%, with a current reading of about 32%.

In Figure 5, note how the implied volatility for options on General Motors stock has ranged from 20% to 82%, with a current reading of about 67%.

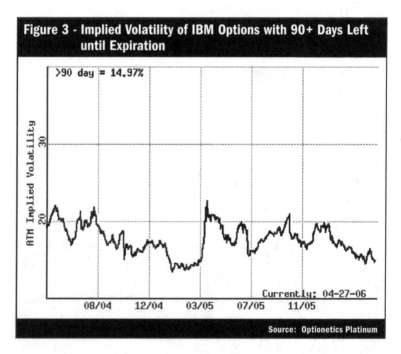

Figure 3 - Implied Volatility of IBM Options with 90+ Days Left until Expiration

Source: Optionetics Platinum

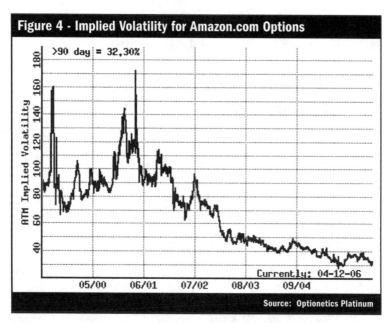

Figure 4 - Implied Volatility for Amazon.com Options

Knowing whether the current level of implied volatility is relatively high or low for the options of a given underlying security is a key element in long-term option trading success. This, in

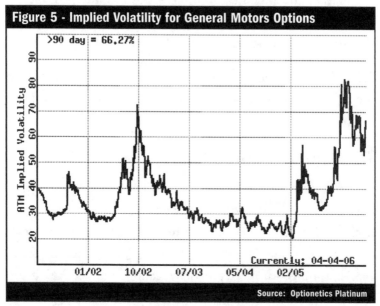

Figure 5 - Implied Volatility for General Motors Options

turn, will tell you if there is a lot of time premium presently built into the option prices for a given security.

WHY MISTAKE #1 CAUSES LOSSES IN THE LONG RUN

There are two primary problems with relying solely on market timing to trade options:

> A) First, picking tops and bottoms for a given underlying security is extremely difficult at best. In fact, many would argue that it is impossible to do on a regular basis.

> B) Second, the movement of the price of a given option is not always directly proportional to the price movement of the underlying security. As a result, even if you pick the exact low point for a given stock or futures market and buy a call option, it is still quite possible that the call option you buy will not generate a big profit, and in fact, might actually lose money.

These facts of option trading life are summarily dismissed by the market timer and are major problems among this group of option traders.

The Market Timing Flaw

For our purposes here, we will define "market timing" as attempting to time an entry and/or an exit into or out of a position—be it a stock, an option, a futures contract, or the stock market as a whole—at the most advantageous time possible. Market timing—or more precisely, accurate market timing—is the "holy grail" of trading. Virtually every investor in the markets engages in some form of timing whether consciously or unconsciously. Even investors with a very long-term perspective who buy and sell stocks based on their expectations of the fundamentals for the underlying company over the next several years still hope to buy at the "right" time. And it makes sense to pursue accurate market timing since the lower you buy and the higher you sell, the more profit you garner on each trade. Still, if you step back and consider all of the material available regarding market timing—including books, articles, newsletters, web sites, hotlines, videos, etc.—you come to realize that not everything works equally well. If it did, every investor would be wildly successful. And that is far from the case.

There is a multitude of potential pitfalls associated with market timing. To start with, there are virtually an infinite number of timing methods currently available and even more waiting to be developed. So the process of zeroing in on a useful method can involve a lot of work on the part of each individual investor. Secondly, not all timing methods are suited for all investors and traders. There are day-trading methods that are based on 1-minute bar charts, which require constant attention. At the other end of the spectrum, methods that are based on long-term trends need only to be monitored on a very infrequent basis. And then there is, of course, everything in between.

Once an investor does settle on a timing method, there is the question of how much patience he or she will maintain if that method suffers a period of underperformance. Even the best trading methods can and will occasionally go for a period of time without generating new profits. That is simply the nature of the trading markets. So the issue at hand for the investor using any given technique is simply, "What do I do when things go sideways, or even down for a longer period of time than I had expected?" One of the most common mistakes that even disciplined, systematic traders make is to abandon their well thought-out trading approach at exactly the wrong time. It is easy to envision how this can happen.

Consider an individual who decides to devote himself to developing a profitable trading technique. He spends days or weeks or months and countless hours determining the optimum criteria for entering and exiting trades. Once the criteria are set and the hypothetical trading results are deemed acceptable, he then begins watching the technique in the markets in real time. For awhile things go very well. Pleased with the real-time results, the trader decides to "take the plunge" and begin trading using his newly developed technique.

For a while things may continue to go well. But, as with all things when it comes to trading, eventually his trading technique goes flat for awhile. After a period of maybe a couple of months of not making any new profits, the trader begins to get a little restless and starts to question if something is "wrong" with his trading technique. Then suddenly, out of the blue, the bottom drops out—even if only temporarily—and the trader begins to lose money at a much faster clip than he is mentally prepared for. At first, he decides to "hang on" in hopes that things will turn around. Ultimately, the fear of losing even more money overcomes him and our trader decides to "pull the plug" in order to stop the pain. So he stops trading using his technique. And if he is like many other traders, in the next few days, weeks, or months, he will watch his technique begin to work well again, quickly earning back the money that had previously been lost and garnering new profits. But while the system itself is doing well, the trader is left behind, afraid to jump back in now that he has "missed the bounce."

Another common problem among investors who actively utilize timing is the tendency to overrate their ability to time the market. No matter how "accurate" a trader believes his or her market timing method to be, the probability of a given underlying security moving in the predicted direction between the time an option is purchased and the expiration date for that option is exactly 50/50. This fact of probability is true even if you are using a trading system that has been 80% accurate in the past.

This statement has stirred some debate in the past and is not accepted by many ardent traders. Still, consider this question: Pick any stock listed on any exchange and ask, what is the probability that this stock will be higher in one day, one week, or one month from right now? The true odds are always 50/50. So despite the fact that 80% of the previous buy signals from a given system or method have been followed by a price advance, the initial probability of the underlying security rising after the next buy signal remains exactly 50/50. Thus, the ardent market timer enters each trade with the flawed perception that the odds are 80/20 in his or her favor, while in fact they are no better than 50/50.

Making matters worse, this probability figure regarding price movement applies to the underlying security itself, not to the options on that underlying security. Option premiums may fluctuate independently based on several factors that are never considered by the market timer, such as time decay and changes in implied volatility.

Underlying Security Price Movement vs. Fluctuations in Option Prices

The implied volatility of an option is a key variable in how an option is priced. While each option trades at its own implied volatility level, the general level of implied volatilities for the options of a given underlying security can fluctuate widely over time. As a result of these fluctuations in implied volatility, at any given point in time, option premiums may be extremely high, extremely low, or anywhere in between. It is essential to your long-term success to be able to determine whether the current level of implied volatility is high or low for a given underlying security. Lack of this knowledge is the key reason that market timers lose money trading options. At times, they pay far too much when buying options because they commit one of the cardinal sins of option trading: they assume that the price movement of the option they buy will mirror the price movement of the underlying security. Adopting the attitude that "any old option will do" is a sure way to lose money on options.

Ideally, you will focus your option buying on situations in which implied volatility is relatively low and focus your option writing (selling) on situations where implied volatility is relatively high. By so doing, you can profit not only from a favorable price movement by the underlying security but also from a favorable change in volatility. The importance of avoiding option purchases when implied volatility is extremely high cannot be overstated.

Anytime you buy an option, a subsequent decline in volatility can cause losses in your option position. In some cases, this can be true even if the underlying security moves in the forecasted direction. This is true whether volatility is high or low at the time you buy an option. However, the higher the implied volatility at the time an option is purchased, the greater the downside risk. It's one thing to be walking down the street and trip and fall, but if you are standing on a mountain top and you trip and fall, then that is something completely different. Clearly, if you are standing at the top of a mountain, you would likely pay close attention to your footing. The market timer who pays no attention to implied volatility levels runs the risk of not only falling off of a mountain top, but of not even knowing he is standing on the mountain top at the time he falls. Ignorance clearly is not bliss.

Less Favorable Risk/Reward Relationship

One factor that is often overlooked when buying options is the expected relationship between risk and reward. Since the probability of making money on a long option position if held until expiration is always less than 50% (because of the inevitable time decay of option premiums as they approach expiration), it is very important to a trader's long-term success that he or she make a lot of money when correct. In other words, if your probability of making money on each trade is less than 50/50 and you always have a risk-to- reward ratio of 1 to 1, then you will lose money in the long run. As a result, it is extremely important to hit a big winner from time to time in order to offset the inevitable losses and allow profits to accumulate over time.

This emphasizes the importance of putting the odds as much on your side as possible for each trade. Unfortunately, the trader who completely ignores implied volatility cannot possibly know whether or not he or she is maximizing the risk-to-reward potential.

Most traders simply expect to make a lot of money any time they buy an option, so they tend to have an overly optimistic idea about their potential reward. Since the purchase of a call option comes with limited risk, they figure that the upside potential is great and the likelihood of losing the entire premium is extremely low. As a result, the perceived risk-to-reward ratio is generally much higher than it actually is in the market place. Let's look at a real-world example.

Most new option traders are trained by prior experience to trade the underlying security rather than the option. When starting out, most traders learn something about technical analysis and/or fundamental analysis. All of this analysis is geared toward determining when to buy or sell a given stock or futures contract. When the decision is made to trade an option on a given underlying security rather than the underlying security itself, many traders mistakenly assume that as long as their timing is good, they can simply buy a call or put and that the option will trade exactly as the underlying does. This type of thinking is actually at the heart of the problem.

In reality, an option trader's work has only just begun once the timing decision has been made. At this point, the trader must decide which option to buy and/or how to manage the position once it is established. If a trader has two or more underlying securities to choose from, the decision becomes even more complicated. As most traders do not have unlimited capital, very often they find themselves in a situation where they may have to choose between trading one underlying security or another. Making the proper selection among different underlying securities and determining which option strategy to employ and which option or options to trade is the step that separates profitable option traders from the other 90%.

Real-World Example

1. On April 6, a trader's market timing method gives buy signals on two stocks, Merrill Lynch (MER) and General Motors (GM).

2. Based on these signals, both stocks are expected to rise 10% in the next month.

3. In order to maximize profitability, the trader decides to buy a call option on one or the other.

4. The trader has $2500 that she wants to commit to one trade.

The question is: Which stock offers the better option play? If the trader has no tools other than her market timing method, she has no choice but to flip a coin or make a subjective guess. The trader who looks beyond market timing can make a much more enlightened decision that will give her a much greater

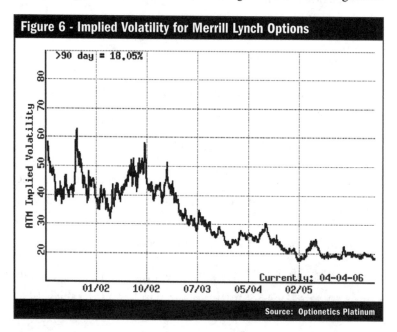

Figure 6 - Implied Volatility for Merrill Lynch Options

>90 day = 18.05%

ATM Implied Volatility

Currently: 04-04-06

01/02   10/02   07/03   05/04   02/05

Source: Optionetics Platinum

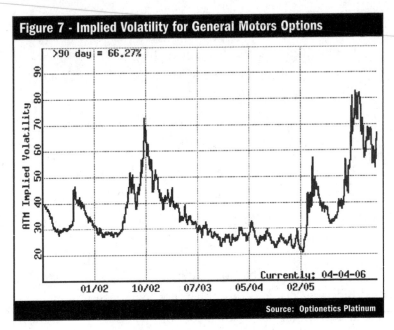

Figure 7 - Implied Volatility for General Motors Options

Source: Optionetics Platinum

profit potential. Figures 6 and 7 display the implied volatility levels for both stocks on the date in question.

Plugging in the following scenario:

1. $2500 of capital.

2. Expecting a 10% advance in price over the next month.

3. Evaluating only "buying calls."

Figures 8 and 9 display the top trades for each stock if the expected scenario plays out—i.e., if Merrill Lynch and GM both rally 10% in the next month. These expected returns are exactly in line with what we would expect.

If Merrill Lynch rallies 10% in the next month, the May 80 call stands to gain 299%. On the other hand, if GM rallies 10%

Figure 8 - Expected Returns for Merrill Lynch Options

Platinum Option Trade Search on: 2006-04-06

Rk	Stock	Click trade below for Options Analysis	Stock Price	Cost	Max Profit	Max Risk	Prob Of Profit	Odds	Days	Vol	Open Interest
1 ☐	MER	Buy 1 MAY06 80 Call@ 2.20	79.91	$220.00	Unlimited	$-220.00	33.93%	0.8 to 1	43	799	2078
2 ☐	MER	Buy 1 OCT06 85 Call@ 2.70	79.91	$270.00	Unlimited	$-270.00	27.86%	1.0 to 1	197	12	1597
3 ☐	MER	Buy 1 JUL06 80 Call@ 3.60	79.91	$360.00	Unlimited	$-360.00	35.57%	0.9 to 1	106	4346	6301
4 ☐	MER	Buy 1 JAN07 85 Call@ 4.00	79.91	$400.00	Unlimited	$-400.00	30.52%	1.0 to 1	288	232	7270
5 ☐	MER	Buy 1 JAN08 95 Call@ 4.60	79.91	$460.00	Unlimited	$-460.00	25.71%	1.1 to 1	652	0	418

Source: Optionetics Platinum

Figure 9 - Expected Returns for GM Options

Platinum Option Trade Search on: 2006-04-06

Rk	Stock	Click trade below for Options Analysis	Stock Price	Cost	Max Profit	Max Risk	Prob Of Profit	Odds	Days	Vol	Open Interest
1 ☐	GM	Buy 1 MAY06 20 Call@ 1.45	19.55	$145.00	Unlimited	$-145.00	30.16%	0.8 to 1	43	3438	11819
2 ☐	GM	Buy 1 JUN06 20 Call@ 2.05	19.55	$205.00	Unlimited	$-205.00	30.27%	0.8 to 1	71	233	29036
3 ☐	GM	Buy 1 SEP06 22.5 Call@ 2.10	19.55	$210.00	Unlimited	$-210.00	25.97%	1.0 to 1	162	155	14474
4 ☐	GM	Buy 1 JAN07 25 Call@ 2.15	19.55	$215.00	Unlimited	$-215.00	24.98%	1.4 to 1	288	136	87493
5 ☐	GM	Buy 1 JAN08 30 Call@ 2.60	19.55	$260.00	Unlimited	$-260.00	24.62%	2.5 to 1	652	161	25603

Source: Optionetics Platinum

in the next month, buying the May 20 call—the top available trade—will gain only 34%. Clearly, traders have much greater potential to get the most bang for their buck trading MER options as opposed to GM options.

One other factor to consider that makes Merrill Lynch options even more attractive in this situation is the fact that the MER option volatilities rise and fall fairly regularly. As a result, one additional benefit of buying options when implied volatility is low is that there is the possibility that implied volatility will rise during the life of the trade, which will inflate the prices of all options for that security. Conversely, if you buy options when implied volatility is high, there is always the danger that implied volatility will decline or even collapse during the life of the trade, thus depressing the price of the option by reducing the amount of time premium built into the option.

For the sake of illustration, let's assume that the implied volatilities for both Merrill Lynch and General Motors regress to their mean—i.e., both revert to the volatility level that is halfway between their high and low readings. For this to happen, Merrill Lynch volatility would rise to 40%. Conversely, GM volatility would fall from 63% to about 50%. Under this scenario, if the option volatility of both stocks reverted to their mean, the upside potential would be even that much greater for Merrill Lynch options compared to General Motors. The profit potential for the Merrill Lynch May 80 call rises from 299% to 320%. Meanwhile, the profit potential on GM May 20 call drops to just 25%.

At this point, it should be clear that not all option trading opportunities are created equal. This example illustrates the importance of not relying solely on market timing to trade options. In this example, the outlook for two different stocks was equally bullish, yet the trader who bought Merrill Lynch call options had much greater upside potential by virtue of buying "cheap" options and the potential for a bigger rise in option volatility. In contrast, the trader who bought General Motors call options had much less upside potential. There is also the risk that implied volatility will revert to the average, or worse, fall into lower territory, thus deflating all GM option prices.

HOW TO AVOID MISTAKE #1

Market timing can be an essential part of option trading success. Unfortunately, the mistake that too many traders make is that they fail to recognize that there is more to option trading success than just market timing. If you do not give serious consideration to which option you choose to buy and how much you are willing to pay for it, you will set yourself up for losses that could easily have been avoided. Not only is this kind of trading obviously bad for your trading account, but the experience of making a good market timing call and still losing money can be extremely damaging psychologically.

Many option traders start out by trading stocks or mutual funds first. While there is much to be learned by doing so, the problem is often that many unwary option traders view option trading as the same game as buying and selling stocks. This is simply not the case. Let me illustrate this point as simply as possible. When you buy 100 shares of stock and that stock goes up in price one point, you make $100. If it goes down a point, you lose $100. If you sell short 100 shares of stock and it goes down one point, you make $100. If it goes up one point and you are short 100 shares, you lose $100. It is a simple straightforward process. If you are long, and the stock goes up 1%, you make 1%. If it goes up 10%, you make 10%; if it goes up 50%, you make 50%, etc. This type of straightforward computation does not necessarily apply to option trading. In option trading, there is any number of additional factors that can play a role in affecting a trade's profitability. Such variables include the strike price (or strike prices if entering into a spread) that you choose to use when entering a trade, the amount of time left until those options expire, the current level of implied volatility, and any subsequent changes in implied volatility after you enter the trade.

If you buy a far-out-of-the-money option, typically the underlying security must make a very large move simply to reach the breakeven price let alone to show a meaningful profit. If you buy an option with one month left until expiration, but the move that you are expecting takes two months to actually occur, you could end up being correct about your expectations yet still end up losing 100% of the capital you committed to the trade. Likewise, as I have illustrated in this section, if you buy an option that is trading at an extremely high-implied volatility, and that volatility level falls significantly after you enter the trade, the amount of time premium in the option that you bought may also collapse.

In order to avoid this mistake, you must make a commitment to go the extra step once your market timing mechanism has generated a signal. That extra step involves determining whether implied option volatility is presently high or low for the underlying security and determining which option trading strategy to employ based on this information. One useful technique is to compare the current level of implied volatility with the historical range of volatility for the particular security you are considering to objectively determine whether the current level is high or low.

In sum, in order to be successful in trading options over the long run, you need to be educated about the critical factors that affect options and option positions. Market timing is only one part of a much bigger picture.

The Concept of Relative Volatility

The concept of Relative Volatility ranking allows traders to objectively determine whether the current implied volatility for the options of a given stock or commodity is "high" or "low" on a historical basis. This knowledge is key in deter-mining the best trading strategies to employ for a given security.

A simple method for calculating Relative Volatility is simply to note the highest and lowest readings in implied volatility for a given security's options over the last two years. The difference between the highest and lowest recorded values can then be cut into ten increments, or deciles. If the current implied volatility is in the lowest decile, then Relative Volatility is "1." If the current implied volatility is in the highest decile, then Relative Volatility is "10." This approach allows traders to make an objective determination as to whether implied option volatility is currently high or low for any given security. They can then use this knowledge to decide which trading strategy to employ, as shown in the following tables (Table 2, 3).

Table 2 - Relative Volatility/Strategy Table

Relative Volatility Rank (1 - 10)

STRATEGY	PROFIT POTENTIAL	RISK	1	2	3	4	5	6	7	8	9	10
Buy Straddles	Unlimited	Limited	X	X								
Buy Naked Options	Unlimited	Limited	X	X	X							
Backspreads	Unlimited	Limited	X	X	X	X	X					
Buy Verticals	Limited	Limited	X	X	X	X	X					
Calendar Spreads	Limited	Limited	X	X	X	X	X					
Sell Verticals	Limited	Limited						X	X	X	X	X
Sell Double Verticals	Limited	Limited							X	X	X	X
Buy Ratio Spreads	Limited	Unlimited								X	X	X
Sell Naked Options	Limited	Unlimited									X	X
Sell Straddles	Limited	Unlimited									X	X

Table 3 - Relative Volatility/Trading Strategy Reference Table												
Relative Volatility Rank (1 - 10)												
HEDGING STRATEGY	PROFIT POTENTIAL	RISK	1	2	3	4	5	6	7	8	9	10
Buy Underlying/ Buy Put	Unlimited	Limited	X	X	X							
Short Underlying/ Buy Call	Limited	Limited	X	X	X							
Buy Underlying/ Sell Call/Buy Put	Limited	Limited				X	X	X	X			
Short Underlying/ Sell Put/Buy Call	Limited	Limited				X	X	X	X			
Buy Underlying/ Sell Call	Limited	Limited								X	X	X
Short Underlying/ Sell Put	Limited	Limited								X	X	X

As you can see in the implied volatility graphs displayed in this section, implied option volatility can fluctuate widely over time. Traders who are unaware of whether option volatility is currently high or low have no idea if they are paying too much for the options they are buying (or receiving too little for the options that they are writing). This lack of knowledge costs them money in the long run.

Mistake #2
Buying Only
Out-Of-The-Money Options

There are three main uses of options. Each use offers exceptional opportunities and specific risks to investors; all three are unique to options trading. In other words, you cannot derive these benefits from trading stocks or futures alone. The three primary uses of options are:

1. Leveraging an opinion on market direction.
2. Hedging an existing position (or generating income from a stock portfolio).
3. Taking advantage of a neutral situation.

While each of these three uses represents a useful opportunity for investors, the majority of traders who enter into the options market—especially those who fail in the long run—do so for the express purpose of generating speculative profits. The irony is that what they set out to do is in fact possible via option trading. The problem is the way in which they go about attempting to achieve these goals.

Before explaining why this is so, let's first cover a few basic but critical concepts. Buying an option gives a trader the right to control 100 shares of stock or one futures contract, typically for far less money than it would cost to trade the underlying security itself. If a trader's timing is correct when entering an option trade, he or she can obtain a much higher percentage rate of return than could be achieved by simply trading the underlying security—with a much lower risk of investment dollars. In fact, by purchasing a call or put option a trader can potentially make the same dollar profit and a much higher percentage rate of return than could be made by committing the capital to buy or sell short the underlying security itself. So for those who fail to profit from buying options, the problem is not the strategy itself, but rather the way the strategy is executed.

Unlike buying a stock that has some tangible value (i.e., a piece of ownership in a company), too many option traders perceive options to be more in line with a lottery ticket rather than an investment vehicle. In other words, the underlying mentality is the "let's take a shot" mentality. In fact, this is so common that without even doing any research one can surmise, with a great degree of confidence, that this approach is definitely a loser in the long run.

There is nothing wrong with the idea of using leverage to attempt to increase one's gains. In fact, the desire to use the maximum leverage available is easily understandable. We all want to make as much money as possible, right? So why not use as much leverage as possible and go for the biggest gains? In a nutshell, the problem with this approach is that too many investors wind up using too much leverage.

The trade-off that needs to be considered is this: the less leverage you use, the higher the probability of a profit being achieved but the smaller that profit will be. Conversely, the more leverage you use, the lower the probability of a profit but the greater the potential gain. The mistake that so many traders make is to apply the greatest leverage possible, hoping for "the big win," without properly considering this tradeoff between profit potential and probability of profit.

Consider this: how many people get rich playing the lottery or make a lot of money in the long run betting on horses or playing blackjack? Perhaps, a few make bank. But the vast majority of players take their shots, get some expensive excitement, ultimately absorb their losses, and move on. This is also the case with option traders who focus solely on long-shot bets by only purchasing out-of-the-money options (and/or options with little time left until expiration). Let's examine this approach a little more closely to understand why this is a losing approach.

WHY TRADERS MAKE MISTAKE #2

Everybody loves a bargain. Something that can be bought cheaply is rightly or wrongly often perceived to be a bargain. Also, many people love betting on a long shot; the idea of making a small bet on a long shot for the possibility of a big payoff is simply an exhilarating prospect for a lot of people. Unfortunately, while this approach to speculation may generate a lot of excitement while the play is being made, in most cases—whether horses, blackjack, or options—it invariably leads to losses in the long run. If your primary purpose for speculating truly is to make money, then you must go out of your way to avoid this "lottery syndrome" and should generally avoid long-shot bets.

> ***Note:*** Before proceeding it should be pointed out that the purpose of this discussion is not to say that you should never "take a shot" in option trading by purchasing a cheap out-of-the-money option. The purpose is to point out that if this approach makes up the bulk of your trading activity, the odds are overwhelming that you will lose money in the long run.

If you had a choice between betting $200 for the chance of making $1,000, or betting $200 for the chance of making $500, which would you choose? Without any more information to go on, the first choice seems an obvious one. A surprising number of option traders take this minimal amount of information and make the "obvious" bet, buying the option with the greater leverage. However, the information that is missing from this example is the probability of achieving the hoped-for return. And this probability is the key ingredient in determining long-term profitability.

Using the example above, let's assume that you have a choice between:

1. Betting $200 and having a 10% chance of making $1,000.

2. Betting $200 and having a 50% chance of making $500.

This scenario presents an individual with an interesting choice. Choice B has a five times greater likelihood of generating a profit; however, Choice A represents the higher maximum profit potential. Well-educated investors could debate this question ad nauseum. While Choice B seems to be the more prudent choice (and is mathematically the correct choice), Choice A still offers a tempting opportunity to anyone who happens to be feeling "lucky" at the time. And unfortunately, too many option traders feel lucky too much of the time.

To better understand the pitfalls associated with the "long shot" approach to option trading, let's cover some definitions, and then look at an example.

- **In-The-Money Option:** A call option is "in-the-money" if its strike price is less than the current market price of the underlying (ITM = call strike < underlying price). A put option is "in-the-money" if its strike price is higher than the current market price of the underlying. (ITM = put strike > underlying price).

- **Out-Of-The-Money Option:** An option that currently has no intrinsic value. A call option is "out-of-the-money" if its strike price is higher than the current market price of the underlying (OTM = call strike > underlying price). A put option is "out-of-the-money" if its strike price is lower than the current price of the underlying (OTM = put strike < underlying price).

- **Intrinsic Value:** The amount by which an option is in-the-money. An out-of-the-money option by definition has no intrinsic value.

- **Extrinsic Value (or Time Premium):** The price of an option less its intrinsic value. The entire premium of an out-of-the-money option consists of extrinsic value, or "time premium." Time premium is essentially the amount that an option buyer pays to the option seller (above and beyond any intrinsic value of the option) to induce the seller to enter into the trade. All options lose their entire time premium at expiration. This phenomenon is referred to as "time decay."

Hypothetical Example

On January 31st, XYZ stock is trading at $55 a share and there are three call options available. The March 50 call is trading at $6, the March 55 call is trading at $3, and the March 60 call is trading at $1. The 50 strike call is "in-the-money" with $5 of intrinsic value and $1 of time premium. The 55 strike call is "at-the-money" and presently has no intrinsic value and is comprised solely of time premium. The 55 strike call will gain one point of intrinsic value for each point that XYZ stock rises above 55. The 60 strike call is "out-of-the-money," has no intrinsic value, is comprised solely of time premium, and will not gain any intrinsic value until XYZ stock trades above $60.

Assume that you are bullish on this stock and expect an advance in price in the weeks ahead. The obvious question then is "which is the better option to buy?" The response to this question varies, but the thought process is almost universal. Each

Table 4 - March Call Options					
Stock (XYZ) Trading @ 55 March Call Options					
Strike	Profit Price	Delta	Intrinsic Value	Time Premium	Price at Expiration*
50	6	82	5	1	5
55	3	50	0	3	0
60	1	26	0	1	0

* If stock price is still $55 at option expiration

trader makes a subjective determination as to which option is best without thoroughly examining the risk/reward character-istics of each choice. The "shooters" invariably like the 60 call because it only costs $100. "The most I can lose is $100, what a deal" is their mantra. The opportunity to buy something at a low price is almost too much for some people to pass up. And so it is in option trading. Very often, when a trader is looking to buy an option, there is an overwhelming temptation to buy a far out-of-the-money option simply because the cost of the option is so cheap. The trader figures, "If I'm right, I'll make a killing; and if I'm wrong, I'll only lose a little." Unfortunately, because this approach completely ignores probability, nine times out of ten it is the trader who gets killed in the long run if this is his primary strategy for trading options.

There are many factors to consider other than just the raw price of a given option. In this example, an investor must con-sider not only the price of each option, but also the likelihood that each option will expire in–the-money. Keep in mind that this table only looks at options for the month of March. The stock might also trade April, June, and September expiration options. Each of those options will also have unique charac-teristics that an astute trader might consider before deciding which one to buy. For example, a June option of a given strike price will cost more than a March option with the same strike price. However, while it will cost a trader more to buy a June option, he or she also has roughly another 90 days of time available for the stock to make a move big enough for the option to generate a profit.

WHY MISTAKE #2 CAUSES LOSSES IN THE LONG RUN

Not everything that seems to be a bargain actually is one. The danger in buying something simply because of its low price is that all too often "you get what you pay for." The primary problem with buying far out-of-the-money options is that you may be inadvertently stacking the odds against yourself.

Probability is an extremely important factor in option trading success. When buying an option, traders can approximate the probability that the option they are purchasing will expire "in-the-money" by checking the "delta" value for the option they are purchasing. A "delta" value is calculated by an option pricing model for each individual option. The delta value can range from 0 to +100 for calls and from 0 to –100 for puts. The significance of a particular option's delta value can be viewed in three different and instructive ways:

1. The delta value for a given option approximates the probability that the option will expire "in-the-money." Thus, an option with a delta of 20 presently has about a 20% probability of expiring in-the-money. While this is not, technically speaking, mathematically precise, it nevertheless serves as a useful proxy. It is also valuable for purposes of comparison. Clearly an option with a delta of +60 is far more likely to expire in-the-money than an option with a delta of 20.

2. A delta value of +20 implies that if the underlying stock increases one full point, the option will increase in value by 0.20.

3. A delta value of +100 indicates that the option position is currently the equivalent of holding 100 shares of stock (or being long one futures contract). Thus, buying a put option with a delta of –40 means the position is equivalent to being short 40 shares of the underlying stock (or being short four tenths of one futures contract).

A delta value of +50 for an at-the-money call option indicates that there is approximately a 50/50 chance that an option will be in-the-money at the time of option expiration. Accordingly, in-the-money call options have deltas greater than +50 and out-of-the-money call options have deltas less than +50. In-the-money put options have deltas between –50 and –100 and out-of-the-money put options have deltas between –1 and –50.

Referring back to our earlier example using XYZ stock, the 50 call had a delta of +82, the 55 call had a delta of +50 and the 60 call had a delta of +26. This tells us that there is an 82% probability that XYZ stock will be above $50 when the March options expire, a 50% probability of being above $55 and only a 26% probability of being above $60. To put it another way, there is a 74% chance that the 60 call option will expire worthless. Make no mistake about it—these are long odds to overcome. Unfortunately, this crucial information is often overlooked or easily dismissed by the trader who has adopted the "what the heck, the most I can lose is $100" approach.

To make matters worse for the shooter, the delta value only measures the probability of the underlying stock reaching the strike price for the option, not the probability that a profit will be achieved. Since you pay time premium anytime you buy an option, your target price is actually higher when buying calls (lower when buying puts), which in turn reduces even further your probability of showing a profit if the option is held until expiration. For example, buying the 60 call option in our example for $1 (or $100) means that your effective breakeven price for the underlying stock is $61 (the 60 strike price + the option premium). The probability of the stock being at $61 or higher by March option expiration (in this example) is just 19%.

To spell it out, if you buy the 60 call for $1, you have less than a 1 in 5 chance of breaking even (before commissions) if you hold this option until expiration. That statement of the facts graphically illustrates what is at the heart of Mistake #2. If the bulk of your option trading involves making bets with less than a 20% probability of profit, the odds are overwhelming that you will lose money in the long run.

To fully drive home this point, let's do some additional math. If four out of every five trades lose $100, then you must make $400 on the fifth trade simply to stay even. Refer again to our example; XYZ stock would have to rise to $65 at expiration in order for the 60 call bought at $1 to generate a $400 profit (this example excludes commissions that raise the bar even higher in the real world of trading). Based on the historical volatility of the stock itself, the probability of this stock reaching $65 at the time of March option expiration is only 8%. Good luck.

Let's discuss one last issue on this topic just to cover all of the bases. The common defensive retort of a shooter after being presented with these facts is to say, "Well, I don't plan to hold the option until expiration. I'm going to hit a big winner and get out quickly." For argument's sake, let's examine this line of thinking. Let's assume that the trader entering this March call trade on January 31 wants to be out by February 28th. Based on computer testing, XYZ stock would have to be above $57.90 on that date in order for the 60 call to show a profit (before commissions). What is the probability of this stock, currently trading at $55, rising to $57.90 four weeks later? In this case, the probability is 28%. So, in sum, while this probability value will vary based on the volatility of the underlying stock in question, in many cases, the hope of simply breaking even still amounts to a long-shot bet.

The best case scenario for the shooter is an immediate movement in the anticipated direction by the underlying security. In order for the 60 call in this example to generate the $400 profit that the trader needs to make in order to cover the $100 he loses on his four out of five losers, XYZ would need to advance to $58 by February 7th. Again, based on the typical historical fluctuations for this stock, the probability of this type of price move happening is just 12%.

Real-World Example

At times, buying options just one strike price apart can make the difference between profit and loss. On April 6th, Apple Computer (AAPL) stock was trading at $71.24.

Table 5 - AAPL May Options				
April 6—Apple Stock (AAPL) Trading @ $71.24 May Call Options				
Strike	Price	Intrinsic	Time Value	At Expiration*
70	5.10	1.24	3.86	1.24
80	1.50	0.00	1.50	0.00

* If stock price is still $71.24 at option expiration

A trader who is bullish on Apple stock may consider one of three possible trades:

- Buy 100 shares of Apple stock (cost = $7,124).

- Buy 14 May 70 call options (cost = $7,140).

- Buy 47 May 80 call options (cost = $7,050).

The shooter is immediately drawn to the prospect of buying the 80 call. By doing so, he can buy more than three times as many options as if he bought the 70 call. This gives him the greatest profit potential if Apple stock rallies sharply. However, with options there is always a trade-off. The trade-off between buying an in-the-money option and an out-of-the-money option is this:

- The out-of-the-money option always offers greater leverage if the underlying security makes a major price move in the anticipated direction.

- The in-the-money option always offers a higher probability of making money than the out-of-the money option.

The factors that the "shooter" who immediately jumps at the out-of-the-money option fails to consider are:

- The real probability of the best-case scenario working out.

- How the worst-case scenario will affect the position.

Take a look at Figures 12 (page 40) and 13 (page 41). These charts display the profit/loss curves for the 70 call option and the 80 call option at expiration, respectively. The price of the stock is plotted along the left-hand side of the graph next to the stock price bar chart. The dollar profit or loss is plotted at the bottom on the right-hand side of the graph. There are several important factors to note when comparing these two positions. The 80 call clearly has the greatest upside potential if Apple stock rallies sharply. Unfortunately, if that is the only factor that a trader takes into consideration, he'll miss several other key factors.

In Figure 10, you will note that the upside breakeven price for the 70 call is $75.10. Based on the actual historical volatility of Apple stock, the probability of Apple being above this price at the time of option expiration is approximately 34%. In Figure 12, you will note that the upside breakeven price for the 80 call is $81.50. Based on the actual historical volatility of Apple stock, the probability of Apple being above this price at the time of option expiration is only about 16%.

The trader in this example must decide which is more important: greater upside potential or a higher probability of profit. There is no exact right or wrong answer to this question. However, the problem is that too many traders never ask this

Figure 10 - Long Apple 70 May Call

	Apple Computer Inc. (AAPL) Option Trade Stock News											
Leg Date	Position	Num	OptSym	Expire	Strike	Type	Entry	Bid/Ask	Model	IV %	Vol	OI	Days
04-06-06	Bought	14	QAAEN	MAY06	70	Call	5.1	5/5.1	5.021	44.0	9190	11679	43

Entry Debit (Cost)	Profit	Max Profit	Max Risk	Delta (Shares)	Gamma	Vega	Theta
$7140.00	$-140.00	$Unlimited	$-7140.00	826.93	51.748	$133.03	$-73.01

Downside Breakeven	Upside Breakeven	Max Profit/Max Risk	Max Profit/Cost
75.10	75.10	Unlimited%	Unlimited%

Source: Optionetics Platinum

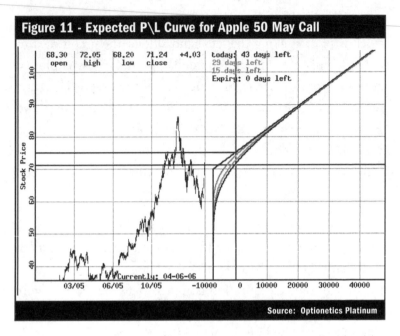

Figure 11 - Expected P\L Curve for Apple 50 May Call

| 68.30 open | 72.05 high | 68.20 low | 71.24 close | +4.03 | today: 43 days left 29 days left 15 days left Expiry: 0 days left |

Currently: 04-06-06

Source: Optionetics Platinum

question at all! They simply go for the greatest leverage with no regard for the other important factors that may affect this trade.

Now let's assume that between April 6 and May 19 (the expiration date for the May options), Apple stock rallies 10%, from 71.24 to 78.36. Let's look at how a trader would have fared under these different scenarios.

Figure 12 - Long Apple 80 May Call

Apple Computer Inc. (AAPL) Option Trade Stock News

Leg Date	Position	Num	OptSym	Expire	Strike	Type	Entry	Bid/Ask	Model	IV %	Vol	OI	Days
04-06-06	Bought	47	QAAEP	MAY06	80	Call	1.5	1.45/1.5	1.475	43.6	3948	2128	43

Entry Debit (Cost)	Profit	Max Profit	Max Risk	Delta (Shares)	Gamma	Vega	Theta
$7050.00	$-235.00	$Unlimited	$-7050.00	1170.91	142.084	$364.53	$-191.47

Downside Breakeven	Upside Breakeven	Max Profit/Max Risk	Max Profit/Cost
81.50	81.50	Unlimited%	Unlimited%

Source: Optionetics Platinum

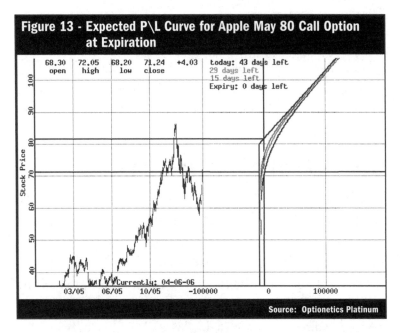

Figure 13 - Expected P\L Curve for Apple May 80 Call Option at Expiration

Source: Optionetics Platinum

Scenario #1) Buy 100 Shares of Stock

If a trader had simply bought 100 shares of Apple stock, he would make $712 on an $7,124 investment—that's a percentage profit of 10%.

- [(stock exit price – stock entry price) x $100], OR

- (78.36 – 71.24) x $100 = $712

- $712 ÷ $7,124 = 10%

Scenario #2) Buy 14 May 70 Calls

If a trader had bought fourteen 70 calls he would make $4,564 on an $7,140 investment—that's a percentage profit of 64%.

- {[(stock exit price – strike price)—option entry price] x 100} x # of calls, OR,

- $\{[(78.36 - 70) - 5.10] \times 100\} \times 14 = \$4,564$

- $(\$4,564 \div \$7,140) = 64\%$

This illustrates the possibility of leveraging your gains using options. However, the danger with using leverage is that you may employ too much as in Scenario #3.

Scenario #3) Buy 47 May 80 Calls

If a trader had bought forty-seven 80 calls at $1.50 each, he would lose $7,050, or 100% of his investment. He would have suffered this loss had Apple closed at the time of option expiration at any price at or below $80 a share. So in this case, despite the fact that the stock rose 10% in about a month and a half, the shooter who went for the most leverage strictly because it was available, suffered a complete loss of 100% of his investment.

Now had Apple stock advanced to $85 or $90 a share by May expiration, things would of course look much different. But the important point to understand here is this: it is acceptable to use a lot of leverage if you truly expect a given security to make a particularly large move and you fully understand the potential for losing money if a move of the magnitude that you expect does not occur.

HOW TO AVOID MISTAKE #2

The trap that many option traders fall into is that they feel that their best move in trading options is to obtain the maximum amount of leverage possible. In other words, "I'm trading a speculative vehicle for the purpose of leveraging my gains, so I might as well go for the gusto." It is almost an irresistible urge that many people get from time to time—that urge to bet on a long shot. Unfortunately, if that approach is standard operating procedure then it invariably leads to losses in the long run. The good news is that the answer to this problem is really very simple. The bad news is that the answer essentially "rains on the parade" of a lot of traders who start out trading options with the notion of earning extraordinary profits.

The Great Paradox of Option Trading

In the long run, one way to make money on long options is to avoid trying to make all the money in the world in the short run. In sum, the key is to use a reasonable and appropriate amount of leverage.

Time decay is the one factor that can potentially hurt all option buyers. A quick review shows that in-the-money options are comprised of intrinsic value—the amount the strike price is below (call) or above (put) the current price of the underlying—and extrinsic value (a.k.a. time premium). At-the-money and out-of-the-money options are comprised solely of time premium. Keep in mind that every option— call or put—will completely lose its time premium by expiration. Consider the implication of this for the buyer of an out-of-the-money option: anytime you buy an out-of-the-money option, you are putting yourself into a situation whereby the underlying security absolutely, positively must move in your favor far enough to be in-the-money by the time of option expiration, or you stand to lose 100% of your investment. In sum, a trader needs to be right or lose 100% of the option premium. While this fact should give most traders a reason to pause, many investors fail to grasp the importance of this trading reality.

If you buy an at-the-money option and hold it until expiration you generally have about a 1-in-3 chance of breaking even before slippage and commissions. Most traders would be better off reducing their leverage and buying options that have some intrinsic value, rather than just buying cheap out-of-the-money options that will more often than not expire completely worthless. In an interview in *Technical Analysis of Stocks and Commodities* magazine, Larry McMillan (the author of *Options as a Strategic Investment* and *McMillan on Options*) advocated buying options with a delta of 70 or more, rather than buying cheap options comprised solely of time premium, which will likely expire worthless. His suggestion was to treat options more like a substitute for the underlying security. Remember that the higher the absolute value for an option, the more closely its price movements will track the price of the underlying security.

A trader looking at XYZ stock, trading at $55 a share would have to put up $5,500 to buy 100 shares of stock (or $2,750 if purchased on margin). As an alternative, the trader could buy the 60 call option for $100, thus obtaining leverage of 55-to-1. This sounds pretty exciting until you remember that the trader only has about a 1 in 5 chance of making money on the trade. Another choice would be to reduce the amount of leverage while greatly increasing the probability of making money. By purchasing the 50 call option for $600, the trader still obtains substantial leverage over simply buying the stock—leverage of about 9-to-1. Also, once the stock rises above $56, the trader would make a point-for-point profit with the stock as it advances higher. Unfortunately, too many investors pass up leverage of 9-to-1 (which when you stop to think about it, is a huge amount of leverage) with reasonably good odds, to "shoot for the moon" with the option offering leverage of 55-to-1 despite the overwhelmingly unfavorable odds.

Because of the negative effects of probability and time decay when buying options, in the long run you stand a much greater chance of trading profitably by reducing your lever-age and buying options with some intrinsic value rather than always "taking shots" with out-of-the money options.

Mistake #3
Using Strategies That Are Too Complex

The majority of option traders who fail to make money in the long run fall into the "market timing is all I need" and/or the "buy cheap options for maximum leverage" traps. However, there are other approaches to option trading that seem to lure in a particular type of trader. While many traders find alluring the prospect of buying cheap options in the hopes of making untold sums of money, others mistakenly assume that if a particular option trading strategy is "complex," it must therefore be "better." This is a dangerous notion.

Option trading offers numerous opportunities to traders, speculators, investors, and hedgers. For example, an option position can make a profit from a number of possibilities including when a stock:

- Rises above a given price;

- Stays below a given price;

- Stays above one price and below another price; or

- Moves above one price or below another price.

In theory, the numerous ways that options make money is a positive thing since it offers investors a tremendous amount of flexibility to craft positions designed to achieve specific objectives. However, with all of this flexibility comes a certain level of complexity. A "complex" strategy can be defined as any trade that involves more than one option, or an option and a position in the underlying stock. Defining the point at which a strategy becomes "too complex" can only be determined on an individual basis. A strategy that is "too complex" is simply one that a trader utilizes without fully understanding either how a profit is made or the intricacies of the risks involved. In the long run, an uneducated option trader is ultimately a danger to himself and his trading account.

WHY TRADERS MAKE MISTAKE #3

The lure of entering into a trade using some specialized strategy and enjoying not only the potential for profit but also low risk is a very tempting idea. In fact, there's nothing wrong with using a complex strategy as long as you fully understand when and how to use that strategy as well as the any potential ramifications due to a situational change after entering the trade. The greatest danger in this realm is the danger of the "neat idea" syndrome. In this case, what typically happens is that the trader starts out simply buying calls and puts, or perhaps writing covered calls. Eventually, the trader learns about another complex strategy and his interest is aroused.

Once a trader learns the basic mechanics of a given strategy—be it a straddle, backspread, calendar spread, butterfly spread, bear call spread, bull put spread, or one of several other choices—he may decide to "give it a try." In most cases, he'll decide to start using whichever of these newfound strategies strikes his fancy the most, rather than learning the optimum situation for utilizing each strategy.

So a trader might start entering into straddles (i.e., the simultaneous purchase of an at-the-money call and put) with the correct notion that he can achieve unlimited profit if the stock goes up or down far enough. An example of this strategy using options on IBM is depicted in Figures 14 and 15.

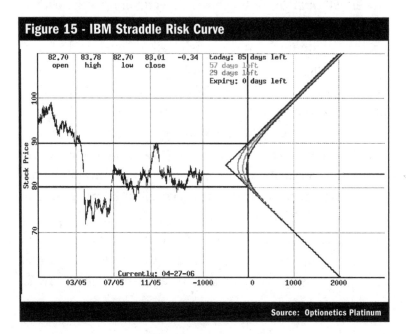

Figure 14 - IBM Straddle Trade

International Business Machin (IBM) Option Trade <u>Stock News</u>

Leg Date	Position	Num	OptSym	Expire	Strike	Type	Entry	Bid/Ask	Model	IV %	Vol	OI	Days
04-27-06	Bought	1	IBMGQ	JUL06	85	Call	1.7	1.6/1.7	1.615	13.6	554	29196	85
04-27-06	Bought	1	IBMSQ	JUL06	85	Put	3.1	3/3.1	3.301	15.1	26	11986	85

Entry Debit (Cost)	Profit	Max Profit	Max Risk	Delta (Shares)	Gamma	Vega	Theta
$480.00	$-20.00	$Unlimited	$-479.93	-12.75	14.357	$31.55	$-2.36

Downside Breakeven   Upside Breakeven   Max Profit/Max Risk   Max Profit/Cost

Source: Optionetics Platinum

Figure 15 - IBM Straddle Risk Curve

82.70 open	83.78 high	82.70 low	83.01 close	-0.34	today: 85 days left 57 days left 29 days left Expiry: 0 days left

Currently: 04-27-06

03/05   07/05   11/05   -1000   0   1000   2000

Source: Optionetics Platinum

As you can see in Figure 14, a long straddle involves buying a call option and a put option with the same strike price and the same expiration month. While the maximum risk is limited to the cost of both options, the maximum reward is unlimited to the upside above the upside breakeven and limited (as IBM can only fall to zero) below the downside breakeven.

The risk graph in Figure 15 (see page 49) shows that the trade will make money if the underlying stock moves far enough in either direction to exceed the downside or upside breakeven points (80.20 and 89.80 respectively), and will lose money if the stock remains between these two prices.

Without a thorough understanding of when to enter a straddle, the uneducated trader may enter into a straddle despite the fact that the implied volatility for the long options are at the high end of the range for that particular security. As a result, the trader will pay a lot of time premium and thus vastly increase his dollar risk (and likewise reduce the trade's probability of profit). In addition, a trader might fail to consider the likelihood that the underlying stock will actually make a move large enough to generate a meaningful profit. Also, because he or she has not thoroughly considered the reward and risk characteristics of this strategy, the new straddle trader may find himself taking profits quickly rather than waiting for a meaningful profit to accumulate. In the meantime, other straddle trades go nowhere as the underlying stocks fail to move enough to generate a profit. After several months of sitting and watching these trades evaporate (as time decay eats away at the prices of the long options), the uneducated trader may decide that straddles "simply don't work," and will choose to foreswear straddles and move on to something else.

Perhaps the uneducated trader, having learned from his experience with straddles that stocks often trade within a range, may decide to try using a neutral option strategy next. Sideways or range-bound strategies make a profit when the underlying security remains within a particular price range. The calendar spread strategy falls into this category. A calendar spread is established by buying a long-term option at one strike price and simultaneously selling a shorter-term option of the same strike price. An example of this strategy using options on Eastman Kodak (EK) appears in Figures 16 and 17 (page 52). This trade involves buying ten July 27.5 strike price calls and simultaneously selling ten May 27.5 strike price calls.

The calendar spread is a very useful and viable strategy. Unfortunately, if the trader doesn't fully understand the implications of this strategy, he may encounter some unanticipated problems. For example, as you can see in Figure 17 (page 52), a calendar spread is indeed a "neutral" strategy, (i.e., it generates profits when the underlying security remains within a given price range). In the Eastman Kodak calendar spread, the downside and upside breakeven points are 25.75 and 29.96, respectively. With no understanding of when to use this strategy, the uneducated investor may inadvertently start trading

Figure 16 - Eastman Kodak Calendar Spread

	Eastman Kodak Company (EK) Option Trade Stock News											
Leg Date	Position	Num	OptSym	Expire	Strike	Type	Entry	Bid/Ask	Model	IV %	Vol	OI	Days
04-27-06	Sold	10	EKEY	MAY06	27.5	Call	1	1/1.05	1.022	38.4	25	5660	22
04-27-06	Bought	10	EKGY	JUL06	27.5	Call	1.65	1.6/1.65	1.628	29.9	113	8389	85

Entry Debit (Cost)	Profit	Max Profit	Max Risk	Delta (Shares)	Gamma	Vega	Theta
$650.00	$-100.00	$777.27	$-650.00	33.79	-43.601	$25.56	$15.57

Downside Breakeven	Upside Breakeven	Max Profit/Max Risk	Max Profit/Cost
25.75	29.96	120%	120%

Source: Optionetics Platinum

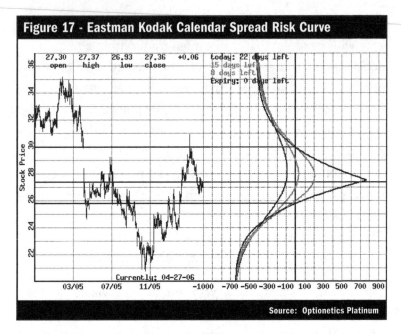

Figure 17 - Eastman Kodak Calendar Spread Risk Curve

Source: Optionetics Platinum

calendar spreads on highly volatile stocks that are fluctuating wildly. This is exactly the opposite of the optimal conditions for placing a calendar spread.

Likewise, because this trader understands little about implied volatility and the implication of changes in implied volatility after a trade is entered, the trader may not realize that buying a long-term option when implied volatility is extremely high exposes him to the risk of a "volatility crush." A volatility crush occurs when the implied volatility of a long-term option declines sharply, thus causing a tremendous amount of time premium to evaporate from the price of the option.

After watching a few stocks soar or collapse outside of the profit range, and/or suffering a couple of volatility "crushes," the uneducated trader may then decide that calendar spreads also "don't work" and will move on to yet another "neat" strategy. And so on and so forth, until the trader either stops trading altogether or ultimately takes the necessary step of getting educated and learning the proper implementation and management of each strategy.

It is also important to remember that not all strategies are the same, even when they have similar characteristics. Consider the following two strategies; both are entered into as a delta neutral position with a combined position delta of zero. (See Mistake #2 for a discussion of option delta values.) A short strangle involves selling a far out-of-the-money call and a far out-of-the-money put with roughly equivalent deltas (call delta values are positive and put delta values are negative; thus selling a call with a delta of +10 and a put with a delta of –10 results in a delta neutral position). A long synthetic straddle is another delta neutral approach that combines the purchase of 100 shares of stock (a position which has a delta of +100) and the purchase of two at-the-money put options, each with a delta of –50. The combined position delta equals zero (+100 – 100 = 0).

Despite the fact that both of these examples represent delta neutral trades, they are very different positions indeed. The first trade (the short strangle) will be profitable if the underlying security remains within a particular range of prices. The second trade (the long synthetic straddle) will profit only if the underlying security moves far enough in one direction or the other to exceed the upside or the downside breakeven points.

In Figures 18 and 19 (page 54), you can clearly see that the risk characteristics of both strategies could hardly be more different, despite the fact that both of these positions start out at (approximately) zero deltas.

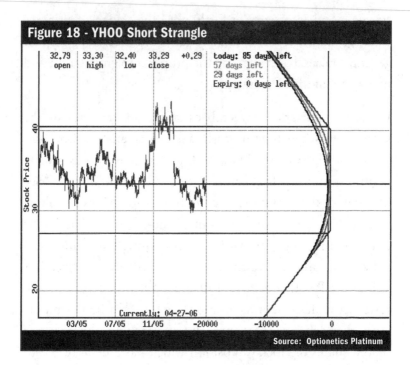

Figure 18 - YHOO Short Strangle

Source: Optionetics Platinum

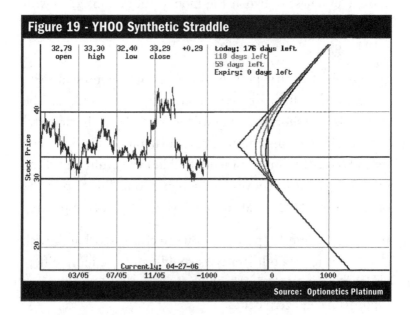

Figure 19 - YHOO Synthetic Straddle

Source: Optionetics Platinum

WHY MISTAKE #3 CAUSES LOSSES IN THE LONG RUN

There is absolutely nothing wrong with trading "complex" option strategies. In fact, the proper implementation of these strategies can be extremely lucrative. The problem occurs when traders start entering into multi-layered positions without first fully understanding the implications of the following important factors:

- The ideal situation for implementing a given strategy.

- The changes that may occur along the way if price and/or volatility fluctuate.

- The ways in which the position might need to be adjusted based on price and/or volatility changes.

- The risk/reward dynamics involved.

To illustrate this point, let's consider an example. One "complex" strategy that occasionally (and mistakenly) gets touted as "low risk" (which is ironic, given the fact that it entails the assumption of unlimited risk) is a strategy known as a short strangle. The typical risk curve for this strategy is shown in Figure 18. This strategy involves selling an out-of-the-money call option and an out-of-the-money put option and then hoping that the underlying security stays within a particular price range so that the options expire worthless. Those who tout the use of this strategy say that it has a "90% probability of profit." And, in fact, that claim may be entirely true, because selling a call with a delta of $+10$ and a put with a delta of -10 can place you into a position that indeed has a 90% probability of profit. In other words, based on the historical fluctuations of the underlying security, there may be a 90% probability that at the time the options expire, the underlying security will either be above the put option strike price or below the call option strike price, thus resulting in a profitable trade.

Many conservative traders are drawn to this type of approach because of the favorable odds. However, if you fail to properly examine the risk/reward dynamics of this trade, you may not realize that you are entering into a trade that has a limited profit potential (limited to the amount of premium you collect when you write the options), unlimited risk to the upside, and limited (but high) risk to the downside. Additionally, this strategy may require a great deal of margin for your broker to allow you to place and hold the trade. Hence, there are a number of important issues to consider before entering into complex trading strategies such as this one.

There Is Rarely Such a Thing as a "Risk Free" Trade

At least not at first.... After you are in a particular trade and have generated a profit, it is often possible to adjust a trade in such a manner that you can lock in a profit. And every once in a great while option prices may get out of line and an alert trader may be able to enter a trade at a net credit thus essentially locking in a risk-free trade. However, given the technology involved in the options market today and the level of sophistication among professional traders and market makers, these opportunities are typically few and far between. The individual investor should not begin trading options with the notion that he or she can expect to profit consistently from these rare opportunities, let alone make a living from them.

As I stated earlier, everything in option trading involves a trade-off. If you buy a cheap out-of-the-money option, you may have a small dollar risk, but you may also have only a 10% probability of actually making money. On the other end of the spectrum, if you sell a naked out-of-the-money call option you may have a 90% probability of making money, but you also are exposed to unlimited risk if for some unforeseen reason the underlying security makes an explosive move in the wrong direction.

Entering into a trade with a 90% probability of making money is very comforting to many traders. However, once this trade is actually entered, the relevant question is no longer "what is my probability of making money?" The relevant question becomes "what am I going to do if the market moves sharply against me and I am faced with a loss?" If the underlying market rallies sharply, the trader in this example MUST act to cut his loss, regardless of his initial "probability of profit."

Rule of Thumb for option trading strategies and life in general: If it sounds too good to be true, it is.

If You Sell Premium, Slippage and Commissions Will Eat Away At Profits

A number of option strategies attempt to take advantage of time decay by selling options. This can be a very profitable approach as any option that is out-of-the-money at the time of expiration will expire worthless, thus allowing the writer of the option to pocket the entire premium collected. One of the negatives to consider, however, is the effect of slippage and commissions. Slippage is simply the difference between the price at which you expect to be filled and the price at which you actually get filled in the marketplace. If you use a limit order, you are guaranteed to enter the trade at the price that you chose; however, there is also the chance that you will miss the trade entirely if your limit price is not reached. If you are using market orders to trade thinly traded options, slippage can be substantial.

Likewise, commissions can vary greatly from brokerage firm to brokerage firm. While good execution and quality service are important factors in using a particular broker, if you are writing options, you must do everything you can to minimize the amount you pay in commissions. When you write (sell) an option, the premium that you receive represents the maximum amount you can make on that trade. Commissions come right off the top. Thus, the higher the commission rate you pay, the lower your profit potential. So, if you are taking in an amount of premium that represents your maximum profit on the trade, it is critically important to keep slippage and commissions to a minimum so that they do not eat up too large of a portion of your profits.

Do You Have A Clear Objective for Entering the Trade?

A given trade might require the underlying security to rally to a certain level or to remain in a certain range in order to generate a profit. Do you have a reason to believe that this will occur? Also, any time you enter into an option trade, you should know what your breakeven price (or prices in some cases) is for the underlying security. In other words, "this position will be profitable if XYZ stays between 50 and 60." You may also need to know at what point your profit is capped and certainly what your maximum dollar risk is as well as the price the underlying security would have to reach in order to generate unacceptable losses, requiring you to act in order to cut your loss.

Recognize That Adjustments to Position May Be Required

Ideally, you will enter into a trade and then simply wait for your profits to start rolling in. However, it doesn't always work that way. Often option positions must be adjusted if certain risk points are reached. A trade that looks good today may not look so good tomorrow and may require a trader to adjust, or "re-balance," the position by closing out some positions and/or opening others.

This is not an issue to take lightly. With certain types of trading you must be prepared to make adjustments exactly when they are needed. This involves planning in advance for each contingency and, even more importantly, having the discipline to pull the trigger in the heat of battle when the critical moment arrives. Another factor to consider is that each time you adjust a position, you are subject to more commissions and potentially additional slippage. As stated earlier, if the strategy you are using entails limited profit potential, trading costs can significantly reduce your profit potential.

Adjustments May Be Subjective

Here is another potential problem, especially for inexperienced and uneducated traders. Say a trader sells an out-of-the-money call and an out-of-the-money put and decides to adjust the position if the underlying security moves within one strike price of either option. Assume further that the underlying security subsequently rallies to within one strike price of the call the trader sold originally. What should the trader do now? Adjust the position? Sure that was the plan. But what is the "right" adjustment to make? He can close out the entire position; he can close out the calls (possibly at a loss); he can close out the calls and sell further out-of-the-money calls; he can close out the calls and sell further out-of-the-money calls; and he can also close out the puts and sell puts with a higher strike price than those originally sold, or some other variation. There is no one answer that is always "correct."

What it boils down to is this: at the worst possible moment (i.e., when the trade is reaching the danger level), the trader will need to reassess the relative merits of a number of options and make a decision in fairly short order as to how best to adjust his position. This is by no means impossible. It does, however, leave a huge amount of room for error, particularly for a novice trader who originally thought he was entering into a trade that was 90% certain to make money.

The key to making proper adjustments is to learn the proper use of the "greek" values associated with options. These values include:

- **Vega**—The expected change in price for an option given a one-point change in implied volatility. For example, a vega of 0.06 implies that if implied volatility were to rise from 30 to 40, this option would gain 0.60 in value.

- **Theta**—The amount of an option price that is lost in one day as a result of time decay. For example, an option with a theta value of 0.015 will lose a cent and a half of time premium on the current trading day. Theta naturally increases as expiration draws closer and time decay accelerates.

• **Delta**—The expected change in price for an option given a one-point change in the price of the underlying security. For example, a delta of 52 implies that if the underlying stock increases in value by $1.00, this option will gain fifty-two cents in value.

• **Gamma**—The expected change in the delta value for an option given a one-point change in the price of the underlying security. For example, if an option has a delta value of 52 and a gamma of 9, this implies that if the underlying stock gains $1.00 in value, this option will increase in delta from 52 to 61.

A complete discussion of the implications of each of these greek variables is beyond the scope of this book. The important point to take away here, however, is that it is foolish to attempt to adjust existing option positions without a thorough understanding of the greeks.

Failure to Adjust May Lead to One Huge Loss That Wipes Out a Lot of Small Gains

It is not uncommon to hear of a trader who enjoys 90% winning trades for an extended period of time (usually selling far out-of-the-money options for small profits) only to get wiped out by one bad trade because he failed to cut his loss when the market moved against him. The only way to avoid this fate is to have a plan and stick to it.

It Can Be Very Difficult To Keep Break-Even/ Adjustment Points Straight

Under the right circumstances, any strategy can work wonderfully. However, with certain strategies the relevant question is "can you make the commitment to follow this position on an ongoing basis in order to make the proper adjustments whenever they are required?" A trader needs to give himself a very honest answer to this question before entering into this type of trading.

Example Position

**On April 27, June 2006 S&P futures were trading at 1309.10
Trade: Short Strangle
Sell 2 May 1345 Calls @ 155 (Total Delta of –24)
Sell 2 May 1255 Puts @ 230 (Total Delta of +22)
Net Position Delta is –2**

If held until the May options expire on May 19, this trade will show a profit if the June S&P is trading anywhere between 1251.00 and 1348.50 as shown in Figure 20. If June 2006 S&P futures are trading between 1255 and 1345 at May expiration, this trades has a profit potential of $3,850 before commissions.

At the time this trade is considered, there is a 90% probability that the S&P will remain within this profit zone. This is exactly the type of "high-probability, low-risk" trade that entices many traders. A problem can arise, however, when a trader enters this trade banking on a high probability of profit without also analyzing the risk side of the equation.

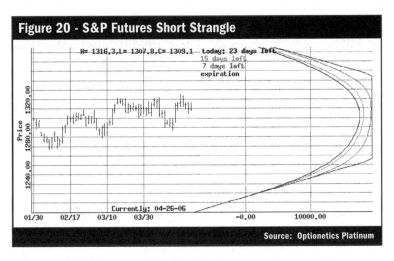

Figure 20 - S&P Futures Short Strangle

Source: Optionetics Platinum

Move Forward One Week

While the profit range seems comfortably wide at the outset, consider what happens to this trade if the S&P futures immediately stage a strong rally.

On May 3rd (one week later), June 2006 S&P futures are trading at 1339.10. The two May 1345 Calls are now trading at 870 with a total delta of −84. The two May 1255 Puts are now trading at 10 with a total delta of +2. Therefore, in just one week's time you went from holding a delta neutral trade with a high probability of profit to a large open loss of $4,950. If the futures keep rising, large unlimited losses can occur!

Consider what just happened. A trader entered a trade that, at least in theory, had a 90% probability of profit if held until expiration. However, because the market made an immediate adverse move, this trader suddenly found himself sitting with a huge loss and now needs to make a critical decision: should he hold on and hope that the market backs off, thus returning his trade to a profitable position (at the risk of experiencing even greater losses if the market keeps advancing)? Or does he immediately cut his loss? These are difficult questions to answer, even for professional traders. The key is to have a plan in place beforehand to deal with adverse situations should they unfold. Traders who use option trading strategies that they do not fully understand run the risk of finding themselves plunged into this type of situation unexpectedly, and then needing to make a critical decision at exactly the most difficult moment.

The key points to remember from this example are:

1. There are NO option trading strategies, simple or complex, that guarantee profits (with extremely rare exceptions), no matter how favorable the initial odds.

2. Every trading strategy has advantages and disadvantages. If you enter any trade for which you are not aware of the potential negative factors involved and/or are unprepared to deal with these negative factors, you are trading with a strategy that is too complex.

HOW TO AVOID MISTAKE #3

As discussed earlier, each individual trader must accurately assess when his or her trading is becoming too complex. The main considerations that you must account for regarding any particular trade or strategy are:

- What is my objective for entering into this trade?

- What is my maximum profit potential and the probability of achieving it?

- What is my maximum risk and the probability of experiencing that?

- Will I need to adjust this position?

- If so, at what point will I need to adjust and what type of adjustment will be required?

- Am I going to be able to keep close enough track of this trade to avoid any potential disasters?

If you cannot answer these questions regarding a particular trade before you enter the trade, then you should not take the trade in the first place. You may know how to drive a car, but you would be ill-advised to get behind the wheel of an Indy race car without first learning more about how to operate it properly. The same is true of option trading. Just because you learn the mechanics for entering and exiting a particular complex strategy, it does not mean you are necessarily prepared to succeed using that strategy. Getting yourself educated to properly implement these strategies is your key to long-term option trading success.

Mistake #4
Casting Too Wide of a Net

One thought that crosses the minds of a lot of option traders goes something like this, "I want to scan every option of every stock and/or futures contract to find the best one to trade." In other words, they believe that looking at every option is the best way to find the best option trades.

WHY TRADERS MAKE MISTAKE #4

At first blush, it sounds like a logical idea. "Certainly if I analyzed every option then I would find the best trades." Unfortunately, there are a number of potential holes in this theory. First, from a psychological point of view, most traders share an unspoken belief that the best trade is "out there somewhere, if only I could find it." Since it can be a time consuming task to scan every option of every stock and/or futures market every single day, it is almost a built-in excuse for some traders to say "if only I could do that, then I would be a winning trader. But since I cannot, there is nothing I can do about it."

WHY MISTAKE #4 CAUSES LOSSES IN THE LONG RUN

In most endeavors, if you try to do too much, you invariably wind up biting off more than you can chew. This reality is also applicable to option trading. The good news is that in option trading you are actually better off if you narrow the focus rather than try to expand it. For example, if you wish to focus on a given strategy and have a clear understanding of the characteristics that should be present in order to offer a good opportunity, then you can use software to scan the universe of options searching for that particular criteria. This type of targeted approach can be highly effective. Let's illustrate this idea with an example.

Calendar Spread Example

As was previously discussed in an example in Mistake #3, a calendar spread is a popular trading strategy and is one that is unique to option traders, as it offers the possibility to make money while the underlying security remains in a neutral price range. To enter a call calendar spread, a trader buys a call option of a given strike price with a longer-term expiration and simultaneously sells a call option with the same strike price but with a shorter-term expiration.

Let's look at an example of a calendar spread. In Figures 21 and 22, we see a calendar spread involving call options for Qlogic (QLGC). The trade shown is entered into by buying ten July 30 calls at $1.30 each, and simultaneously selling ten May 30 calls at $0.80 each. This trade costs $500 to enter. Barring any changes in implied volatility levels, the trade will show a profit at May option expiration if QLGC is trading between the breakeven prices of 18.66 and 21.67.

So, can a trader simply use some sophisticated software to scan every conceivable calendar spread and then put on the trade with the highest profit potential and wait for the profits to roll in? Not necessarily. Yes, a trader can use software to quickly

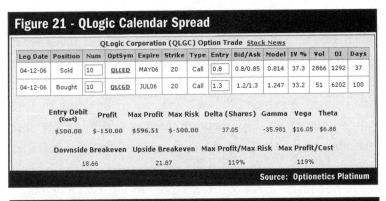

Figure 21 - QLogic Calendar Spread

QLogic Corporation (QLGC) Option Trade <u>Stock News</u>

Leg Date	Position	Num	OptSym	Expire	Strike	Type	Entry	Bid/Ask	Model	IV %	Vol	OI	Days
04-12-06	Sold	10	QLCED	MAY06	20	Call	0.8	0.8/0.85	0.814	37.3	2866	1292	37
04-12-06	Bought	10	QLCGD	JUL06	20	Call	1.3	1.2/1.3	1.247	33.2	51	6202	100

Entry Debit (Cost)	Profit	Max Profit	Max Risk	Delta (Shares)	Gamma	Vega	Theta
$500.00	$-150.00	$596.51	$-500.00	37.05	-35.981	$16.05	$6.88

Downside Breakeven	Upside Breakeven	Max Profit/Max Risk	Max Profit/Cost
18.66	21.87	119%	119%

Source: Optionetics Platinum

Figure 22 - Qlogic Calendar Spread Risk Curve

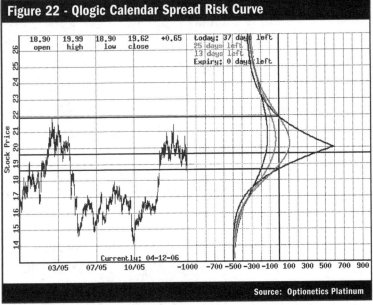

Source: Optionetics Platinum

highlight potential calendar spread trades. However, as with virtually all option trading strategies, there are several factors that must be carefully analyzed and considered before a calendar spread is entered.

One factor to consider is referred to as the volatility "skew." Skew simply refers to the differences in the implied volatility levels for options of different strike prices and/or different expiration months. Since a calendar spread involves buying one option and simultaneously writing another, it makes sense that the ideal situation would involve writing an option that is trading at a much higher implied volatility than the option that is being purchased. By so doing, we are ensuring that we gain an edge by writing an option that has relatively more time premium built into than the option we are buying. A trader who simply looks for the calendar spread with the highest profit potential may completely ignore this important factor.

Another key consideration is the distance between the break-even points (i.e., the width of the profit range). Clearly a calendar spread with a wider price range between the upper and lower breakeven prices has a higher probability of ending with a profit as there is more room for the stock to fluctuate without exceeding the upper or lower breakeven prices. Again, simply scanning the universe for the calendar spread with the greatest profit potential does not take this factor into consideration. And in fact, even if it did, there is even more to this picture than meets the eye.

It is a mathematical fact of option trading life that changes in implied volatility levels have a much greater effect on longer-term options than they do on short-term options. As a result, if a trader enters into a calendar spread that involves buying an option trading at an implied volatility level that is at the high end of its historical range, that trader may be facing a danger of which he or she is completely unaware.

Figures 23 and 24 show a call calendar trade using Rambus options. As you can see in Figure 24, this trade appears to have tremendous profit potential as well as an extremely wide 27.37 point spread between upper and lower breakeven prices (31.32

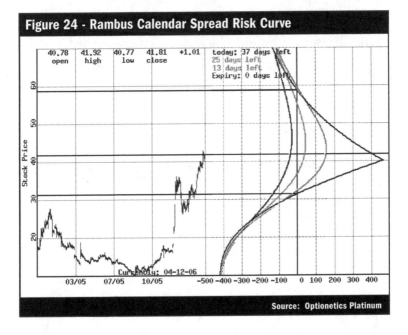

Figure 23 - Rambus Calendar Spread

Rambus Inc (RMBS) Option Trade Stock News

Leg Date	Position	Num	OptSym	Expire	Strike	Type	Entry	Bid/Ask	Model	IV %	Vol	OI	Days
04-12-06	Sold	1	BNQEH	MAY06	40	Call	7	7/7.1	7.063	115.4	343	12876	37
04-12-06	Bought	1	BNQKH	NOV06	40	Call	11.2	10.9/11.2	11.056	78.9	21	708	219

Entry Debit (Cost)	Profit	Max Profit	Max Risk	Delta (Shares)	Gamma	Vega	Theta
$420.00	$-40.00	$466.28	$-420.00	3.70	-0.948	$6.79	$5.98

Downside Breakeven	Upside Breakeven	Max Profit/Max Risk	Max Profit/Cost
31.32	58.69	111%	111%

Source: Optionetics Platinum

Figure 24 - Rambus Calendar Spread Risk Curve

to 58.69). An uneducated option trader looking at this trade might assume that this trade is almost a sure profit.

But when we look at the history of implied volatility for long-term RMBS options in Figure 25, we realize that the call option being purchased in this trade is presently trading at the high end of the historical implied volatility range. So what happens if volatility declines between now and the time the May options, which we are writing, expire? What happens is something that was mentioned in Mistake #3, and is known to knowledgeable option traders as a "volatility crush." As the implied volatility of the longer-term option declines, so does the amount of time premium built into that option. As a result, the entire risk curve collapses to lower ground. In the process, the maximum profit potential declines dramatically and the breakeven points move closer and closer together as implied volatility declines.

In the Rambus example, if we assume that implied volatility were to fall from the present level of approximately 80% to just 60%—a reasonably good possibility as you can see in Figure 25—we can see how the prospects for this trade change between Figures 24 and 26.

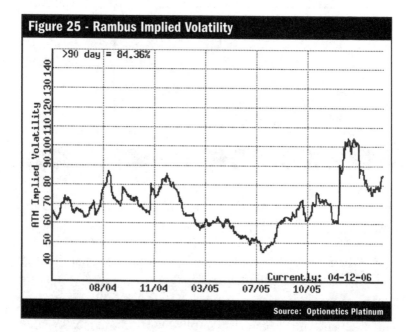

Figure 25 - Rambus Implied Volatility

>90 day = 84.36%

Currently: 04-12-06

Source: Optionetics Platinum

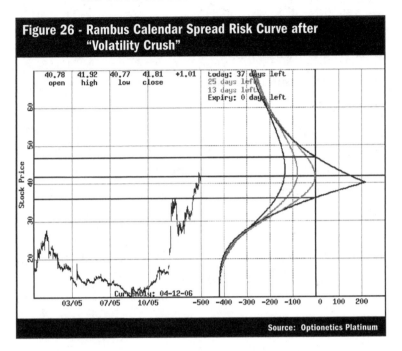

Figure 26 - Rambus Calendar Spread Risk Curve after "Volatility Crush"

Source: Optionetics Platinum

In this example, as a result of a decline in implied volatility from 80% down to 60%, the upper breakeven point falls from 58.69 to 46.74, and the lower breakeven point rises from 31.32 to 35.99. Suddenly, instead of a profit range of 27.37 points, there is now a profit range of only 10.75 points.

This example clearly illustrates the importance of educating yourself about various option trading strategies before actually using them. While software nowadays makes searching for calendar spreads (and virtually any other option trading strategy) relatively easy, unless you know specifically what criteria you are looking for, you may be setting yourself up for unexpected losses.

There are other reasons why "casting the widest possible net" is not necessarily a path to easy profits in options.

You Cannot Look at a Particular Option and Say It Is a Good One to Trade

As the calendar spread example illustrated, it is simply not possible to look at the price of a given option in a vacuum and say, "Yes, this is a good option to trade." Every option will react in a slightly different way to a given move by the underlying security. In order to make a realistic assessment of the benefits of buying or writing a given option, you must have some future scenario in mind in order to properly determine the prospects for a particular trade. This generally involves either some type of market timing forecast or some outlook for a change in volatility levels, either up or down.

Limitations of Analysis of Actual vs. Theoretical

Another common refrain among novice traders is "I want to look at all the options so I can find the most undervalued options to buy (or overvalued options to sell)." What this refers to is the difference between the theoretical price of a given option, which is calculated by using an option pricing model, and the actual market price of the option. If the actual price is below the theoretical price, then the option is considered to be "undervalued." Likewise, if the actual price is above the theoretical price, then the option is considered to be "overvalued." Traders often believe that they can gain an edge by buying "undervalued" options and/or selling "overvalued" options. This is true to a limited extent, but there are a number of caveats involved.

Just because an option is trading below its theoretical value, there is no assurance that it will go up in price. If a particular call is undervalued and the underlying security declines in price and/or volatility declines, the price of the option will decline no matter how undervalued it may appear to be.

Likewise, just because an option is trading above its theoretical value, there is no assurance that it will ultimately decline in price. If a particular call is overvalued and the underlying security advances in price and/or volatility increases, the price of that option will increase no matter how "overvalued" it may appear.

Implied option volatility levels can fluctuate widely over time. Everything else being equal, you are generally better off buying an overvalued option when implied volatility levels are low than you are buying undervalued options when implied volatility levels are extremely high.

Taking advantage of option mispricings is generally best left to floor traders and/or professional market makers who have instant access, minimal trading costs, and can buy at the bid price and sell at the ask price, as well as to arbitrageurs who do nothing but look for such opportunities. The small trader is almost certain to lose in the long run if he gets into the game of trying to take a fraction of a point here and a fraction of a point there out of the option market. Bid and ask spreads and transaction costs will almost invariably negate any advantage that a retail trader might hope to attain.

There are different option pricing models available; Black/ Scholes, Binomial, Cox/Rubenstein, etc., and different models may generate different theoretical prices for the same option. One model may indicate that a given option is overvalued whereas a different model may tell you that the same option is considered fairly valued.

The biggest limitation in considering theoretical option prices is that they don't really matter all that much when you get away from theory and into the real world of trading. For example, say that three different option models generate three different theoretical prices for the same option—5.63, 5.74, and 5.86, respectively. When you go to buy this option in the real world you may find that the Bid price is 5.50 and the Ask price is 6.00. The market makers for that option don't care where you think the option should be priced. If you want to trade this option right now, you can either buy it at 6.00 or sell it at 5.50. Those are your choices in the real world.

Here is the bottom line regarding Actual versus Theoretical option prices. In general, you should try to avoid buying an option that is trading far above its theoretical value and you should also strive to avoid writing an option that is selling far below its theoretical value. Beyond that you should pay far more attention to likely underlying price movements, implied volatility levels, trading volume, and bid and ask prices than to theoretical option prices.

Lack of Trading Volume Makes Many Options Difficult To Trade Efficiently

If you look closely at a newspaper that reports option volume as well as option prices, you will notice something interesting. A lot of options trade very little volume on a daily basis. In fact, many don't trade at all. Still, there is a price quoted for the option. Many traders assume that if the option price is in the paper, it's just as good as any other option in the paper and that they can buy or sell as many as they want at that price.

Unfortunately, the difference between theory and reality can be a chasm a mile wide when it comes to trading. Seeing a price quoted for a particular option and believing that it offers a good trading opportunity can be a far cry from actually going into the marketplace and getting filled at that quoted price. Option market makers often joke about options that trade "by invitation only." What this implies is that you need to "look behind the curtain" and see if there is any trading actually going on in an option that you are looking to trade. When looking at options for a stock or futures market you've never traded before, call your broker and ask for the bid/ask spread on a few options. If the bid/ask spread is wide, you may want to avoid trading in that market.

HOW TO AVOID MISTAKE #4

One thing that should be evident by now in option trading is that if something seems easy or logical, it should probably be avoided altogether, or at least questioned. Most traders do what seems easiest or most logical. What an interesting coincidence that most uneducated option traders lose money in the long run. It seems logical to want to cast a bigger net and try to follow all option trading strategies for all stocks or futures markets in an effort to find "the best trades." But in reality, most traders would be much better off by narrowing the focus, rather than trying to widen it.

To make money in options, you need to learn to spot exceptional trading opportunities. The definition of an exceptional trading opportunity varies from strategy to strategy. Some strategies are best entered when implied volatility is low; others when implied volatility is high. Some spread strategies will make money if the underlying security moves in a particular direction, others will profit if the underlying security remains in a particular price range. Understanding the implications of a particular strategy and the factors that will affect your trade once you enter requires some actual thought on your part, not just an act of mindlessly scanning as many options as humanly possible.

Also, in order to take advantage of a trading opportunity, you need someone to take the other side of your trade at a reasonable price. This requires trading volume. As a result, traders often benefit from focusing their efforts on those stocks and futures markets that offer the greatest option trading liquidity. Figure 27 presents a list of stocks and futures markets that tend to have consistently high option trading volume.

Figure 27 - Stocks & Futures Markets with Active Option Volume

Stocks with Active Option Trading	Futures with Active Option Trading
Amazon.Com	Corn
Apple Computer	Crude Oil
Cisco Systems	Euro FX
Citigroup	Gold
Dell Computer	Heating Oil
eBay	Japanese Yen
Exxon Mobil	Natural Gas
GM	S&P 500
Google	Soybeans
Hewlett Packard	T-Bonds
Home Depot	10-Year T-Notes
IBM	5-Year T-Notes
Intel	
Lehman Brothers	
Merck	
Merrill Lynch	
Microsoft	
Pfizer	
Procter & Gamble	
QUALCOMM	
Rambus	
Texas Instruments	
Wal-Mart	
Yahoo!	

Source: Optionetics Platinum

By focusing on stocks or futures markets with consistently active trading volume, you will probably find more trading opportunities than you can use and you will be able to devote more time to each security than if you tried to cover every available stock or futures market. Just as importantly, you will be able to actually take advantage of these trades in the marketplace. Most traders find a stock or futures market that they want to trade and then look at the options. However, if you plan to trade options actively, you will benefit in three ways if you start by focusing on only those securities that have consistently high option trading volume.

The Benefits of Narrowing the Focus:

There are several benefits to narrowing the focus:

A) You will spend less time trying to sift through every option of every imaginable security looking for that "one great trade" and will have more time to devote to meaningful analysis of a handful of securities.

B) Once you narrow the focus, chances are you will be amazed at how you find yourself discovering more trading opportunities than you can actually use.

C) When the time comes to actually make an option trade, you will find market makers offering a spread of 0.05 of a point rather than 0.20 point or more for illiquid options. This difference alone will save you a great deal of money in the long run.

Another way to "narrow the focus" is to settle on a handful of option trading strategies that you are most comfortable in using. An educated and experienced option trader can easily rattle off the names of ten to twelve different strategies (long call, short call, butterfly, calendar spread, bear call spread, bull put spread, straddle, bull call spread, bear put spread, backspread, etc.). And each strategy has unique advantages and risks associated with it. Ideally, you will master as many strategies as possible in order to have as many "arrows in your quiver" as possible. Nevertheless, in the majority of cases, successful option traders tend to focus on just a handful of strategies with which they are most comfortable.

SUMMARY

The traits most often associated with option trading are limited risk, unlimited potential, leverage, and the ability to tailor a position to fit a particular objective. The good news is that all of these traits accurately portray the opportunities available when trading options. The bad news is that options by their very nature are a complex subject, which leaves a great deal of room for error. In order to succeed, a trader must do the homework required to fully understand what his or her true objectives are and to devise and follow a plan that has a realistic expectation of achieving those objectives. Unfortunately, because of the complex nature of options, many traders find it easier to simply follow the most common approaches to trading without really considering the likelihood of a profitable outcome in the long run. "If everybody else is doing it, it must be right" is a common thought. However, when you are talking about an endeavor where 90% of the participants wind up losing in the long run, the opposite is actually true.

The most difficult step in becoming a profitable options trader is realizing and accepting that the "usual" approaches to option trading followed by the majority of traders lead to losses, and that a trader must ardently avoid the common pitfalls if he hopes to profit in the long run. The table below presents a brief summary of the mistakes we have detailed, why they lead to losses, and what a trader needs to do in order to avoid these problems.

Table 6 - SUMMARY TABLE		
MISTAKE	**WHY THIS CAUSES FAILURE**	**HOW TO AVOID IT**
Relying Solely On Market Timing	Ignores implied volatility; can lead to paying far too much to purchase options	Carefully analyze which option (or options) are best suited to achieve your objective
Buying Only Out-Of-the-Money Options	Ignores probability; leads to buying options with little likelihood of profiting	Consider the likelihood of making money on a given trade before getting in
Using Strategies That You Don't Fully Understand	Leads to unfavorable risk\reward situations	Determine your objective and make certain the trade you are going to make can achieve those objectives without more risk than you can handle
Casting Too Wide a Net	Too much time wasted looking randomly for opportunities	Narrow the focus of the strategies you will consider and the securities you will trade

Option trading can generate substantial profits if you avoid the common mistakes and adopt an intelligent approach. Avoiding the mistakes detailed in this guide is one of the best first steps you can take!

About the Author and Optionetics

Jay Kaeppel is an independent trader and a Trading Strategist for Optionetics, Inc. His weekly column "Kaeppel's Corner" can be read each week at www.optionetics.com. With more than twenty years of experience as a stock, mutual fund, option and futures trader, his expertise as a system developer has been noted by *Technical Analysis of Stocks and Commodities* magazine, which has published several of his articles on such diverse topics as:

- A winning approach to futures trading

- Stock market timing with interest rates

- Stock market timing with the Stock/Bond Yield Gap

- Stock market timing with long-term price momentum

- Bond mutual fund investing and bond market timing

- Gold mutual fund investing and gold market timing

Jay Kaeppel has been featured in interviews in *Technical Analysis of Stocks and Commodities* magazine, *Futures* magazine, and *Barclays Managed Futures Reports*. "Formula Research," a national monthly trading system development advisory edited by Nelson Freeburg, has acknowledged Jay Kaeppel's expertise as a trading systems developer by using two of his original systems as the foundation of their own stock market and gold fund trading systems.

COMPANY INFORMATION:

Optionetics

255 Shoreline Drive, Suite 100
Redwood City, CA 94065

Main Office (8 AM–5:30 PM PST) Telephone

(888) 366-8264
(650) 802-0700
Send us your Success Stories:
testimonials@optionetics.com

International Seminars:
international@optionetics.com

Ask questions about publication or Platinum subscriptions:
pubinfo@optionetics.com

Optionetics Platinum and/or Trading Strategies

If you have questions about how to use Optionetics Platinum
or if you want to report a problem: Platinum Support Forum
http://www.optionetics.com/bbs/forum.asp?forum_
id=10&forum_title=Optionetics+Platinum

For lost passwords, billing information, user names or order-
ing:
platinuminfo@optionetics.com

Please post your trading questions to one of our "Ask the
Traders" boards at our Message Boards http://www.optionet-
ics.com/bbs/default.asp#Ask%20The%20Traders

Trading
Resource
Guide

❖

Tools for Success

in Options Trading

SUGGESTED READING LIST

OPTIONS: A COMPLETE GUIDE FOR INVESTORS AND TRADERS

Guy Bower

This hands-on workbook takes you from the basics to the more compound methods of option trading. Real-world examples, an extensive Q&A section at the end of each chapter, as well as further resources, add to the value of this outstanding guide on options. Get on the road to success by becoming a more effective and profitable options expert now!

300 PP $39.95 ITEM #BCKAEP-3362693

THE LEAPS STRATEGIST: 108 PROVEN STRATEGIES FOR INCREASING INVESTMENT & TRADING PROFITS

Michael C. Thomsett

Unleash the power of Long-Term Equity Anticipation Securities (LEAPS) for increasing gains, limiting losses, and protecting your trading and investing profits. Real-world examples and graphic illustrations in this comprehensible guide, point out the main keys of this book. Not only are LEAPS a low-risk alternative to buying stock, they are also a great way to maximize your capital.

296 PP $34.95 ITEM #BCKAEP-2529875

THE FOUR BIGGEST MISTAKES IN FUTURES TRADING

Jay Kaeppel

Learn to avoid the 4 most common – and costly – mistakes futures traders make that cause them to lose money in the long run. Describes the opportunities and challenges of futures trading, and how the average trader can succeed in futures by embracing 4 key principles of trading mastery.

111 PP $19.95 ITEM #BCKAEP-11190

To order any item listed & MORE...
Go to **www.traderslibrary.com**

THE OPTION TRADER'S GUIDE TO PROBABILITY, VOLATILITY, AND TIMING

Jay Kaeppel

Trade options with confidence - using this expert new guide. Find a variety of strategies to trade options intelligently—and profitably—in any given situation, and the guidance on when to apply them. Covers: • Risk assessment guidelines • Groundbreaking "Risk Curve" analysis • Timely exit methods • Insights into the biggest mistakes option traders typically make—that you can avoid.

271 PP $69.95 ITEM #BCKAEP-84666

AN INTRODUCTION TO OPTION TRADING SUCCESS WITH JAMES BITTMAN

The CBOE's top options trainer introduces first-timers and fledgling traders to the exciting options arena. Bittman explains in concise, step-by-step terms exactly how options work, providing clear explanations and examples of the most common—and valuable—option strategies. With Bittman's basic strategies, discussed in this comprehensive video, your entry into the options market will be far more focused and effective. *Includes complete online support materials.*

90 MN DVD $99.00 ITEM #BCKAEP-3502409

OPTIONS FOR THE STOCK INVESTOR

James B. Bittman

Updated to reflect changes in the options market, this extensively revised second edition features all-new material describing electronic trading, decimalization, and single stock futures, along with increasingly popular vehicles such as stock indexes, LEAPs, and exchangetraded funds. The CD-ROM contains all-new OP-EVAL II software, which eliminates guesswork while providing handson information on spreads, position Greeks, and "what-if" forecasting and graphing features.

256 PP $39.95 ITEM #BCKAEP-3226190

OPTIONS AS A STRATEGIC INVESTMENT, 4TH EDITION

Lawrence G. McMillan

It's the top selling options book of all time. Over 800 pages of exhaustive coverage on every aspect of trading options. Called "the single most important options reference available," this mammoth work teaches you to: track volatility and the key role it plays for traders; learn rules for entering/exiting trades at optimal levels, build a successful trading plan. Plus, must-read sections on LEAPS, CAPS, PERCS and cutting edge risk abatement techniques.

896 PP $80.00 ITEM #BCKAEP-17300

AVOIDING OPTION TRADING TRAPS

Lawrence G. McMillan

Renowned author, Larry McMillan, shows you how to avoid the 5 most common—and costly—mistakes option traders make. Master his methods for using put-call ratios, picking the right option, and deciding how much to risk and so much more. McMillan shows you what to do in typical tough spots—and how to avoid them in the future. This video is "must-viewing" for any investor looking to move beyond the realm of options theory - into the world of option profits.

99 MN DVD $99.00 ITEM #BCKAEP-3374856

To order any item listed & MORE...
Go to **www.traderslibrary.com**

Important Internet Sites

TRADERS' LIBRARY BOOKSTORE — *www.traderslibrary.com*

The #1 source for trading and investment books, videos and related products.

SMARTTRADECORNER — *www.smarttradecorner.com*

Interviews, articles, surveys, book excerpts, webinars and many other trading resources. Connect with other traders and discover new ideas and tested methods.

CHICAGO BOARD OPTIONS EXCHANGE — *www.cboe.com*

Daily market statistics with extensive archives and introduction to options resources.

OPTIONS INDUSTRY COUNCIL — *www.888options.com*

Seminars, webcasts, education and toll free hotline.

OPTIONETICS — *www.optionetics.com*

Education, trading tools, resources and market information.

OPTIONSXPRESS — *www.optionsxpress.com*

The premier online options broker with the most powerful tools for all options traders.

OPTIONS STRATEGIST — *www.optionstrategist.com*

Short-term stock and option trading site on the latest techniques and stratgies for trading a variety of innovative options products.

BIG TRENDS — *www.bigtrends.com*

Daily, weekly and monthly alert services with powerful commentary and actionable insight on the options and stock markets.

At Optionetics®, we show you how to create a steady revenue stream that allows you to do the things in life that matter most.

Our FREE Trading Kit will help you get started.

The Trading Kit is ideal for people with little or no experience in options trading, and includes:

- **Simplify Your Options with Optionetics** – an interactive CD that introduces you to the rewarding world of options trading

- **Getting Ready to Trade Options** – the quintessential must-read before placing your first options trade

"I [made] $60,000+ profit. I paid cash for a Lexus LS430."
- Optionetics student Warren B., Las Vegas, NV

Order your FREE Trading Kit now!
www.freetradingkit.com
or within the U.S. call

888-366-8264
(650-802-0700 internationally)

www.optionetics.com

Best of all, it's FREE.

Over 250,000 people in more than 50 countries have seen Optionetics high-profit, low-risk, low-stress trading strategies in action. Many are realizing their dreams of financial freedom.

You can, too. It's easier than you think.

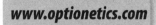

Free 2 Week Trial Offer for U.S. Residents From Investor's Business Daily:

FREE
2 WEEK
Trial Offer

INVESTOR'S BUSINESS DAILY

Power Processors Light Up Internet
Even When All The Lights Go Out

I NVESTOR'S BUSINESS DAILY will provide you with the facts, figures, and objective news analysis you need to succeed.

Investor's Business Daily is formatted for a quick and concise read to help you make informed and profitable decisions.

To take advantage of this free 2 week trial offer,
e-mail us at customerservice@traderslibrary.com
or visit our website at www.traderslibrary.com where
you find other free offers as well.

You can also reach us by calling 1-800-272-2855
or fax us at 410-964-0027.

This book, along with other books, is available at discounts that make it realistic to provide it as a gift to your customers, clients, and staff. For more information on these long lasting, cost effective premiums, please call us at (800) 272-2855 or you may email us at sales@traderslibrary.com.